Greenland - Then and Now

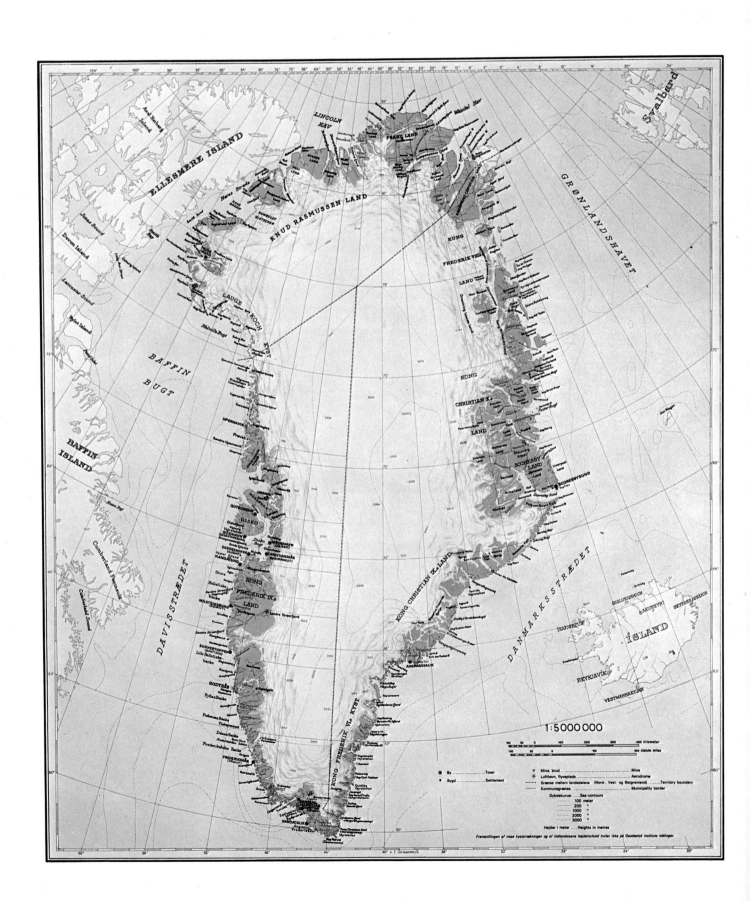

Erik Erngaard

Greenland

Then and Now

LADEMANN

GREENLAND – THEN AND NOW
Design: *Freddy Pedersen*
Translation: *Mona Giersing*

© 1972 by Lademann Ltd.,
Copenhagen

Printed in Finland
ISBN 87 15 08073 0

Preface

Almost a thousand years have passed since the
day when the first European set foot on Greenland's icy rocks. 250 years have gone by since
the colonization of Greenland began - but it is
only 20 years since it ceased to be a colony.
This book shows episodes from the history of
Greenland which can be equalled by no other
area in the world. The narrative of a thousand
years tells of life, then and now, in this border-
land of existence - without pretending to be the
whole thruth about Greenland.

Most of it is White

There are 839,781 sq. miles of Greenland, and out of this, 607,885 sq. mil. are always white. This is the inland ice. The rest is green, brown or white, depending on location and time of year. Here the people live. 45,000 scattered over 131,896 sq. mil. 38,000 are Greenlanders and 7000 Danes.

The 45,000 are spread over a coastal area 25,000 miles long. So they have plenty of room.

The southernmost point of Greenland is called Cape Farewell. The most northernly is Cape Morris Jessup. The distance between these two points is 1660 miles, being equivalent to the distance between Labrador and the Gulf of Mexico. The difference in climate is equally great. In northernmost Greenland and on the inland ice - where temperatures have been measured down to 95° F. below and where variations of 115 degrees might be experienced within a few days - all life is at the extreme margin of existence. Southern Greenland, approximately in the same latitude as Anchorage, has deep fjords with green valleys and something which looks like forests.

Aside from the population, Greenland is the land of the big figures. The biggest island in the world also claims the world's longest fjord, Scoresby Sound, which is at least 185 miles long. It is also the deepest with its 4760 feet. In Jacobshavn the most diligent glacier of the northern hemisphere can be found, sending an iceberg into the ocean every five minutes and annually producing five cubic miles of ice. The inland ice varies in altitude from 5000 feet to 10,500 feet above sea level. The world ocean would rise 23 feet if it melted!

For centuries Greenland has drawn Europeans and Americans like a magnet. In many respects it is still a mysterious country. No other area in the world with such a small population has been described in such great detail as Greenland. To this day more than 35,000 books and papers have been published on Greenland subjects, i. e. almost one book per Greenlander.

And here is another one.

The field ice in Eastern Greenland. It comes from the Arctic Ocean, drifting down along the coast. Here, the waters are navigable only two months of the year

Far left: A typical view of Greenland as may be seen by any visitor to the west coast of Greenland

It is not all ice, however. The short summer is hectic, exploding in a riot of colors—so much has to be accomplished in so short a time

The First People in Greenland

Where did they come from? And where did they go? We don't know. What we do know, however, is that the North Pole had its neighbours as early as 4000 years ago. Many archaeological finds throughout this enormous kingdom of ice, which embraces the Arctic Ocean coasts along the American and Asiatic continents have shown that. In a world, more mild and dry than it is today, they pushed forward along the northernmost

Portrait of a Norseman, a woodcarving made by an Eskimo somewhere between 1100 and 1200. The headgear clearly indicates this, and—maybe–the rather surly mouth. This is the face af a ruler

migration paths toward Greenland and then down along its eastern and western coasts. We call them the Sarqaq people because remains of their culture were found in the Sarqaq Settlement in Disko Bay. They were reindeer hunters and their dogs were enormous – 35 inches at the shoulder. The Sarqaq people were not driven out by other tribes but by the unconquerable Arctic nature.

A new culture was already on its way, however. The Dorset people. They used harpoons, not bows and arrows like the Sarqaq people and they did not have any dogs. The Dorset people walked south along the coasts of Greenland in the paths of the Sarqaq people and very often settled in the same places as their predecessors had done it a thousand years earlier. The memory of the Dorset people still lives on in their self-portraits, carved in walrus tusk, and in the Eskimo myths that called them "the inland people".

While in the wilds of Canada they met another people, the Eskimos, or the sea people, who were much better suited to withstand the climatic changes which began about 500 A.D.

Whether caused by the invincibility of nature or of the Eskimos, the Dorset people vanished, too. It is evident from the Canadian myths that they were fought down by the Eskimos.

About 900 A.D. the Dorset people seem to have disappeared from western Greenland or maybe they withdrew to the bottom of the deep fiords where the reindeer lived. They continued to live for centuries, however, in isolated settlements on the eastern coast of Greenland and possibly they have mixed with the Eskimos. This might explain why the eastern Greenlander looks very different from the western.

Just before the year 1000 A.D., Greenland was once more practically depopulated, but new cultures were on

their way. From the east came the Norse vessels bringing with them a peasant culture and from the northwest the slender kayaks with a hunter culture, the Thule culture.

Where these two cultures met for the first time, no one knows, but it must have happened on the coast of western Greenland, far up north. At Inugsuk near Upernavik, Eskimo sites have revealed various Norse-articles, some clothing and a checker piece. For centuries the two people lived and fought each other on the same land, but always, in peace as in war, the Eskimos came out the victors. The same happened to

This was how the Thule people looked at the time Eric the Red steered his vessels to Greenland. The portrait is carved out of the handle of a scraper and can be dated to the 10th century. The material is walrus tusk

the Norsemen as happened to the Sarqaq and Dorset people: they disappeared into the dusk of history. Only the Eskimos persevered, and today's Greenlanders are their descendants.

It is not known where the cradle of the Eskimo culture stood and their language does not reveal anything certain about their origin. However, their mongoloid descent is indisputable.

They settled anyhow, and nature, however inhospitable in these northern regions, could not displace them. But Danish welfare has effaced their characteristics and that is why we no longer speak of Eskimos, but of Greenlanders, like in the sagas of Iceland where the Norsemen were originally called *Groenlendina,* the Greenlanders.

Thus the dramatic history of Greenland begins with the Norsemen.

The Dorset man wore a high collar and a coat down to his ankles. The figure is carved in walrus tusk and found in the ruins of a house in the Thule district. At right: Dorset woman with hairtop, also found in the same district

The Bloody Road to Greenland

The Skolholt Map, drawn in 1590 by Sigurdur Stefánson. The original was lost but a copy was made in 1670. The datemark on the map–1570–is believed to be a copyist's mistake. From Björn Jonson's "Descriptions of Greenland"

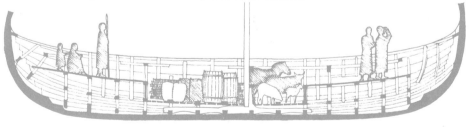

The knarr (or round ship) was not nearly as elegant as the traditional viking ship. This cross section of a trade ship, recovered at Roskilde Fjord, shows how the cargo was kept midships

Almost a thousand years has passed since *Eric the Red's* blood-stained past led him to Greenland; in the year 982 to be exact.

Together with his father, Thorvald, he had to leave Jaeren in Norway for Iceland to escape punishment for manslaughter. The only land available to Eric and his father was the barren northwestern coast of Iceland, since most of the island had been colonized during the past one hundred years.

After his father's death, Eric married the wealthy Tjodhild and built his farm, Eriksstad, at the bottom of Bredefjord. But even here he could not refrain from getting involved in feuds. At first he killed two men and was banished from

This rendering of Eric the Red is made by a 17th century artist from a woodcut in Arngrímur Jónsson's "Groenlandia," 1688. University of Copenhagen

the area. But before he had finished the building of his new farm, he was once again involved in a quarrel, this time with a farmer named Thorgest. A big battle ensued in which many were killed, among them Thorgest's two sons. Eric had to appear before a jury at Thorsnaes Thing, where he was outlawed.

Thus he was forced to leave Iceland, and as he had heard of a land out west, he decided to find it. Nearly one hundred years earlier, another Norseman, Gunnbjörn, had told of this land he had seen when his ship had been put out of course west of Iceland.

Eric found the land. With its deep fjords and lush pastures it was much more pleasant than the barren country he knew in northern Iceland. He named it "Greenland", because he felt that if the country had a good name "people would be attracted thither".

For three years he explored the new land and then returned to Iceland.

In the year 986, he sailed back to Greenland with 25 heavily laden ships an nearly 700 persons on board. Fourteen of the ships arrived safely with their cargoes of men, women, children, horses, cows, sheep and goats. The rest of his followers either turned back or disappeared at Cape Farewell, thus becoming the first of the countless number of people who—over the past millenium—have lost their lives here.

Eric took possession of Eriksford, near the site of the present Julianehaab, and founded Brattahlid, the Eastern Settlement. Other Icelanders sailed further north and set up the Western Settlement in Godthaab Fjord. Thus the greenest part of Greenland was populated and a life began which should last several hundred years. Exactly how long, no one knows, because we have no accounts of what became of these first daring landnamsmen. Their fates are shrouded in the darkness of the Middle Ages.

It was believed earlier that Eric the Red and his followers sailed to Greenland in ships like the Oseberg ship (above). To-day, however, the experts are convinced that he used a knarr like the one found in Skuldelev near Roskilde in 1960 (below)

Some Were "Sea Lost"
- But Others Found Their Way

No one knows for certain how the Norsemen managed to find their way to Greenland. In Norse itmes the traffic between Greenland and Norway was rather brisk –even though this meant covering more than 1650 nautical miles. But how could they cross the Atlantic and return, with no compass?

Captain Carl V. Soelver devoted considerable space to this problem in the Greenland Association Year Book for 1944. He feels that the "Solarsteinn" (sun stone), used by the Norsemen, was a "sun shadow board". At night they sailed by the North Star which they called "Leidarstierna".

In Landnámabók, an ancient Icelandic text from the 9th and 10th century, can be found a description of the route from Norway to Greenland: "From Hernum in Norway sail directly towards the west until Hvarf (Cape Farewell) in Greenland, you have thus sailed northward of Hjaltland (the Shetland Isles), so near that you can see it, if the weather is clear, but southwards of the Faroes, and such that the sea goes towards the brae, and southwards of Iceland."

The description is not very exact, and the sagas often tell of people who were lost at sea. They even had a special word for it: The sailors were *sea lost*. The Flatey Book describes it this way: "But then the rain stopped and they had northernly winds and fog, and they knew not whereto they sailed, and in this manner passed many a day. Thereafter they had sun."

A pelorus. There are several theories as to how this navigational instrument was used. Most experts claim that it rotated around a pin; others say that it floated in a bowl of water with a piece of magnetite at the bottom–in other words, it worked almost like a compass

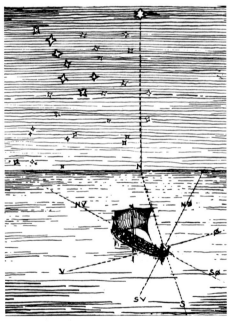

In all probability, the way in which the vikings sailed by the North Star

Taking a bearing in the grey morning. Drawing by Otto Bülow

The Icelandic handwritten sagas form the basis of our knowledge about the movements of the Norsemen. Even though these sagas were written down several hundred years after the actual events took place, they seem extremely correct. This page is from the 3rd chapter in Groenlendinga Saga in the Flatey Book, telling how Eric the Red stumbled with his horse

They Knew Not Bread, but Arthritis

Thanks to the sagas and archaelogical finds, we know a good deal to-day about life in the Greenland of Norse times. Almost 300 persons lived in the Eastern and Western Settlements. Every single green area, even below the steepest mountains, had its farm. Where to-day the sheep are grazing on the Norse ruins and graves, life went on in the same quiet and toilsome way as a thousand years ago. During the short summer they grew grass and grain for their horses, cows and pigs. They did not know bread, only milk and cheese. And what they could not reap from their own peasant culture, the generous Arctic nature gave them: hare, seal, reindeer, whale, salmon and cod. They were dressed in homespun like all other Europeans at that time. In 1921, Dr. Poul Nørlund of the National Museum in Copenhagen made an exceptional find at the Herjolfsnæs churchyard (near the present Frederiksdal): 30 kirtles, 17 hoods, 5 hats and 6 stockings–all deep frozen and much better preserved than the clothing from any other known find. Thus, from these finds in Greenland we learnt how the men and women of Europe were clad: in similar clothing with a so-called liripipe hood of varying length.

Many of Eric the Red's men were over six feet tall, some even taller, and the average height for men was 5ft. 7in. and for women 5 feet. It is easy to understand why they called the squat Polar Eskimos, who pushed down from the north, *Skrellings*. The Norseman's health was excellent and his teeth did not have any cavities. On the other hand, he knew arthritis. Some Norsemen were so bent when they died that they could not be straightened out before being placed in the grave.

The experts found very few infant skeletons in the graves, which was surprising, since, in those times, infant mortality was as a rule very high. The explanation might possibly be found in the Norsemen's rather harsh form of family control–the exposing of newborn children was very common. In Finnboga Saga it is told how the child is placed between two stones with a piece of suet in his mouth and a third stone to cover him. Exposure of children did not stop until long after Christianity was introduced.

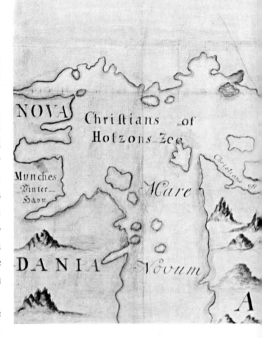

On the earliest maps Greenland was shown landfast with Spitsbergen in Norway. The Eastern and Western Settlements were placed wrongly according to the four quarters of the globe, thus giving rise to the misunderstanding that the Eastern Settlement was located at the east coast of Greenland. This map is from the 17th century

This is the way they must have looked when they stood on the fields of Eric the Red

Life in Norse Greenland was rugged, wild and brutal–like the people. One of the countless Eskimo myths tells of an Eskimo attack on a Norse farm, here illustrated by the Greenlander Aron from Kangek. The Norsemen were having bad luck–only one of them got away, namely a thrall who had been left onboard one of the ships. At the last moment he is able to set sail

A Woman's Weapon
Against a Heathen

Eric the Red was a heathen and the priest–whom his son Leif brought back from Olav Tryggveson, Norway's king–he called a swindler.

Eric's wife, however, believed in the priest's words and let herself be christened. The old landnamsman and murderer most surely grumbled at this, especially when she started to build a church. It as very small, though, eleven feet long and two feet wide, and could hold no more than 20-30 standing listeners. Tjodhild's husband could easily resist all the splendour and glory of Christianity–but according to Eric's Saga, he did not have a chance against woman's age-old weapon: Tjodhild refused to have anything to do with him. Then he gave in.

With this, Catholicism made its entry into Greenland. Strangely enough, it also disappeared again 500 years later with the Norsemen, but the church ruins testify to its importance. In 1124, Greenland got its first bishop; his name was Arnald. He let himself be consecrated in Lund in Sweden, reluctantly though, because he had heard that the people among whom he should work were very troublesome. It went much better than he had expected though.

A cathedral, 81 × 48 feet, was built in Gardar, in the Eastern Settlement. The bishop's farm had a facade of 150 feet and one of the rooms were 24 × 50 feet. The church had become the real power in Greenland.

The head of a crosier cut from a walrus tusk. The crosier was buried in 1209 together with the bishop Smyrill. Below Eric the Red's Brattahlid, where the sheep are now grazing

Hvalsey church, the biggest ruin from the Norse period, situated at the bottom of Julianehaab Fjord. The drawing is made by W. A. Graah who continued Hans Egede's search for the Eastern Settlement. Below. In 1964 this skeleton was dug up at the churchyard of Tjodhild's church. It could be Eric the Red

Wooden crucifix found under a bench at a farm in the Western Settlement

Three crosses from the Norse period. The runic inscriptions on the cross at left tell about the Virgin Mary, God, Our Father and the Son

Everyday Life on the Norse Farms

The many Norse finds from several hundred farms, churches and monasteries have supplied us with considerable information on life during the almost 500 years when the Norsemen lived in Greenland.

The people were fairly self-sufficient, except for wood and iron, which they could not get on Greenland. Their supplies came mostly from Bergen in Norway by the regular shipping connections to Greenland.

Admittedly, the first Norsemen were landnamsmen and bellicose vikings–one find revealed a skeleton with a knife through the chest. But they were also farmers, hunters and fishermen. They made all their own tools and for the keeping of butter and cheese, salt meat and fish they made vessels and bowls out of soapstone, which is quite common in Greenland. This stone is so soft that you can easily cut it, but it is not harmed by fire. Therefore, it is well suited for cooking purposes.

When they were unable to get pig iron, they used the local bog iron. They had forges where axes, knives, spearheads and nails were made. The Norsemen also made their own clothes, using the wool from their sheep. They carded and wove a homespun cloth which they also used for bartering when the ships from Norway arrived. The Greenland homespun was of a much better quality than the European cloth and therefore much in demand. During the winter they made beautiful tools from wood, horn and bone, toys for the children, game pieces for checkers.

From about 1150 until 1400, men and women dressed similarly. The child's dress above with the small skullcap is one of the many finds from the churchyard at Herjolfnæs in the Eastern Settlement

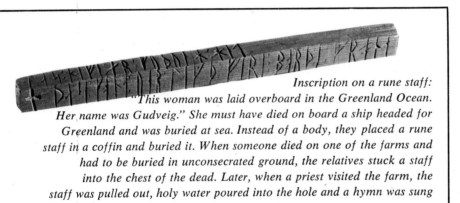

Inscription on a rune staff:
"This woman was laid overboard in the Greenland Ocean. Her name was Gudveig." She must have died on board a ship headed for Greenland and was buried at sea. Instead of a body, they placed a rune staff in a coffin and buried it. When someone died on one of the farms and had to be buried in unconsecrated ground, the relatives stuck a staff into the chest of the dead. Later, when a priest visited the farm, the staff was pulled out, holy water poured into the hole and a hymn was sung

Elaborately decorated soapstone vessel from the Western Settlement. It was probably used in the household on one of the farms

Game pieces for checkers and chess. One way to pass away the long, dark winter evenings while the Arctic storms raged outside

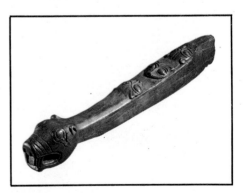

No one knows what this carved wooden piece from the Norse period has been used for. The brief runis inscription reads "Helge". Maybe an armrest for a chair

The most important political event in the Norse period took place in 1260 when the Norwegian king, Haakon Haakonson, united all the colonies in the North Atlantic Ocean, including Iceland, in one kingdom called *Norgesvældet* (The Norwegian dominions).

At first the Icelanders resisted, but finally they surrendered and in 1262 paid tribute to the King at the *Althing*. In return, he pledged to send at least six ships to Iceland every year. The Norsemen had no choice but to follow the example of the Icelanders. They promised to pay fines for homicides.

One hundred years later, when Norway and Denmark were united under the same king, Greenland became part of the union and after its abolition in 1814, Greenland remained a part of the Danish kingdom.

During the years 1931-32 Norwegian whalers occupied several areas in the uninhabited East and North Greenland, and the Norwegian government recognized this occupation as valid. Denmark, however, appealed to the World Court at the Hague, which in 1933 awarded Denmark sovereignty over all of Greenland.

And that's why Greenland is Danish today.

Children's toys have also been found. Below is the handle of a toy sword, a soapstone figurine, a small vessel and a bird made from wood

From Nordsetr–the long stretch from the Western Settlement at Godthaab Fjord to north of Upernavik–the Norsemen fetched some of the things they sold to Europe, in particular furs and narwhal tusks. There is no doubt that sometimes the Norsemen wintered far up north. This runic stone which was found in 1824 in a cairn near Kingigtorssuaq (north of Upernavik) is proof of that. The inscription reads: "Erling Sigvatssón and Bjarne Tordssön and Erinride Oddssön erected this cairn on the Saturday before Rogation Day." This early in the year (in April) Northern Greenland is closed for navigation. The ice does not break up until beginning of June, so the men must have wintered

This bear is carved from walrus tusk and was found at the Sandnæs farm in the Western Settlement. It has a hole in the foot. Maybe it was an amulet

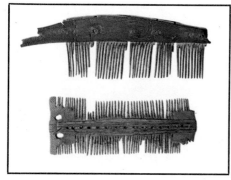

Personal cleanliness was high with the Norsemen. They bathed often and combed their hair. These combs were found in Norse ruins

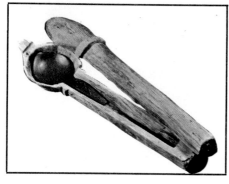

Their spoons of horn were rather brittle and, therefore, were kept in cases as shown here. All the above pieces were found in various Norse ruins

The Voyage to Vinland

It was the Norsemen from Greenland–and not Columbus–who first discovered America. Leif, a son of Eric the Red, and later known as "Leif the Lucky" discovered America, or Vinland as he called it, in the year 1000.

The story about his voyage to America with 35 men, is rendered very accurately, almost like a ship's journal, in the Saga of Eric the Red and in Snorre's Hcimskringla (the sagas of the Norwegian kings). Eric the Red very nearly won the distinction as the dicoverer of Vinland, because Leif had asked his father to be the leader of the expedition. But as Eric was departing from Brattahlid, his horse stumbled, the ageing chieftain fell off and injured his leg. According to his own saga he then said: "I am not destined to discover more lands than the one in which we now live. We shall never sail together again."

Leif and his men reached Vinland, lived there for one year before returning to Greenland, their ships loaded with grapes and wood. During the winter Eric the Red died.

When spring came, Leif's brother, Thorvald, decided to explore Vinland –this time with 30 men. Leif had not met any people in Vinland, Thorvald did, however. On one of the beaches he

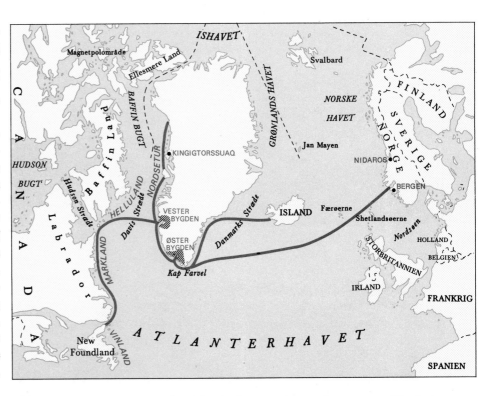

The Norse sea routes across the Atlantic Ocean a thousand years ago. The daring Norsemen traversed these immense distances in their open boats without a compass

One of the proofs in support of the theory that the Eskimos knew the Norsemen. The two wooden figures, made by Eskimos, show Norsemen with liripipe hoods

This is how the land looked when Leif the Lucky discovered America around the year 1000–as the Norwegian painter Christian Krohg saw it. The painting, which hangs at Nasjonalgalleriet in Oslo, gives us an excellent idea of the hardships endured by the Norsemen on their long sea voyage

found three kayaks made of skin, with three men under each. In the usual Norse fashion Thorvald and his men seized their axes and killed all but one, who escaped.

Later, while the Norsemen slept, the natives attacked in great numbers and during the fight Thorvald was mortally wounded by an arrow.

We find many accounts of the Vinland expeditions in the sagas. One of the most fullblooded and shocking is the story of Freydis, a tough wench, who very much resembled Eric the Red, whose illegitimate daughter she was. According to *Flatey Book,* she travelled to Vinland with two Icelanders, Helgi and Finnbogi. They had 30 men on their ship and the agreement was that she should take 30 men on hers. However, she doublecrossed the two brothers by taking 35 men, so that she would be sure to have the upper hand. Their stay in Vinland ended in a violent clash. The Icelanders and all their men were killed, and Freydis herself finished off their women with an axe.

Upon her return to Greenland, she was of course, frowned upon because of her misdeeds. Leif Ericsson, who had become chieftain after his father, did not quite know how to handle the problem. In the end, he ignored the matter completely.

The Norsemen named their newly discovered lands *Markland, Helluland* and *Vinland.* Helluland was the present Baffin Island, Markland was the Labrodor coast and Vinland was Newfoundland. It was on these inhospitable shores that Dr. Helge Ingstad in 1960 found traces of the Norsemen's first visits.

Whatever was known of this new land around the year 1000 disappeared with the Norsemen. And any written material, aside from what is available today, went up in flames when Copenhagen was burnt in October 1728.

The "Vinland Map" which created quite a stir when published in 1965. It was probably drawn by a German monk in a handwritten manuscript, dating from the middle of the 15th century. The experts have serious reservations as to its genuineness, among other things because Greenland is drawn as an island. There is no doubt, however, that its worm holes are authentic. The map belongs to Yale University

This arrowhead, found in 1932 at the Sandnes farm in the Western Settlement by Dr. Aage Roussell, presumably proves the connection between the Norsemen and America. It is believed to be Indian, and it is made from a sort of flint stone which has never been found in Greenland

What Became of the Norsemen?

Towards the end of the 14th century the thin life line with Bergen was severed, and one day there were no Norsemen left in Greenland. Did they emigrate to Vinland? Were they killed by *Skrellings?* Or by pirates? Or did they die from a distinct drop in temperature? The puzzle has never been solved. Unquestionably, they had experienced attacks by English and Scots pirates. This is evident from a letter which Pope Nicholas V wrote to the two bishops of Iceland. The letter tells of gruesome fire attacks on Greenland. The holy buildings were destroyed by fire and sword and the people taken as thralls.

The Norsemen also had to fight the Skrellings. Stories about this appear both in Norse legends and in Eskimo myths. Ivar Baardson from Gardar gives an account of his last visit in 1350 to the Western Settlement: "... when we arrived at the place no people were there, neither Christian nor heathen, only stray cattle and sheep of which we helped ourselves until the ships could hold no more ..." This was the end of the Western Settlement. And soon after the turn came to the Eastern Settlement.

Icelandic legends from 1379 describe the events: "The Skrellings attacked the Norsemen, killed eighteen men and took two boys as thralls." To-day no one considers it very likely that the Eskimos did away with all the Norsemen. Caterpillars may have done it, though. Studies made at the Western Settlement have disclosed dense layers of cocoons. Caterpillars in enormous quantities could have attacked the grass and willow leaves which were used for forage.

But even though the Norsemen had disappeared, they lived on in the dramatic myths of the Eskimos, visualized centuries later by the outstanding Greenland artist, Aron from Kangeq.

Aron's 40 woodcuts and 250 paint-

ings, using motives from the Eskimo myths tell of the arctic dramas which took place in Norse times. They are tales of friendship and enmity.

Among these is the following account of the first Norse attack on the Eskimos.

Up until then, the Norsemen and the Eskimos had lived peacefully side by side. The cause of the quarrel is a wily Eskimo girl by the name of Navaranaq. She is a regular visitor in both camps and succeeds in making bad blood between them. After the fight and the flight of the Norsemen, the Eskimos turn to Navaranaq. "They grabbed her by the arms and dragged her at full speed. Thereupon some of them tied strong thongs to her topknot and her arms and dragged her on her back across the ice. When her back was torn to pieces, they asked her, "Are you having fun, Navaranaq?" And she answered, "Of course I am having fun" —but they dragged her even further, and when the entrails poured out of her back, they asked her once more, "Are you having fun, Navaranaq?" To this she gave no answer."

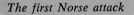

The first Norse attack

The Norsemen have beheaded an Eskimo woman. They have taken the head home to use as a lucky wheel

The Eskimos are thirsting for revenge and prepare themselves for battle

During his flight, the Norse chief throws his child into the water in order to escape

The Eskimos are revenging themselves on Navaranaq

After the voyages to Greenland ceased, the land only existed in oral traditions and on some rather fantastic charts. This Italian chart, dating from approx. 1467, shows the North Atlantic Ocean and Northern Europe. The golden areas and lines indicate glaciers. Greenland has been placed much too close to the British Isles

Far Out West Was a Land...

For almost one hundred years the Norsemen were the only people in Greenland. Attempts were made from Northern as well as Southern Europe to establish a thin life line to them, but in vain. Out west, behind the ice, was a land. That much was known, because the legends of it lived on, even though the charts at that time were very inaccurate. They were useless for navigating - nothing but desk jobs.

In the 15th century the Portuguese were very engrossed in geographical expeditions and twice they asked the Norwegian king to send out Greenland expeditions. Finally, in 1472 or 1473, a ship was heading for the Northwest. In charge were Didrik Pining, Hans Potthorst, Johannes Scolp (a Norwegian) and Juano Cortereal (a Portuguese). It is believed that they arrived at the east coast of Greenland. They were driven away, however, partly by the Eskimos and partly by a storm which carried them all the way to Newfoundland. From there they returned without ever having reached their original destination. The Church, too, tried to reach Greenland. The Archbishop of Trondheim, Erik Valkendorf, raised a subscription in favour of sending out a ship - and in 1492 the Pope tried to send a bishop to Gardar. Both attempts failed. In the meantime much was written and told of the Norsemen and numerous charts were drawn. As time went on, a good many things were distorted and the Eastern Settlement shifted to the east side of the Greenland map. For centuries the ships kept running their bows right into the ice masses on East Greenland in their attempts to find a settlement which only existed in the magination of the cartographers.

The Danes also made a few attempts. In 1521 King Christian II let shipmaster Sören Nordby equip a ship, but, it never made sail, this despite the fact that the good Nordby had had the foresight to secure absolution from the Pope in anticipation of the possible debauchery of the crew! The Pope had to wait almost 450 years, before he was able to send a Catholic priest to Greenland.

He settled in an American military tent.

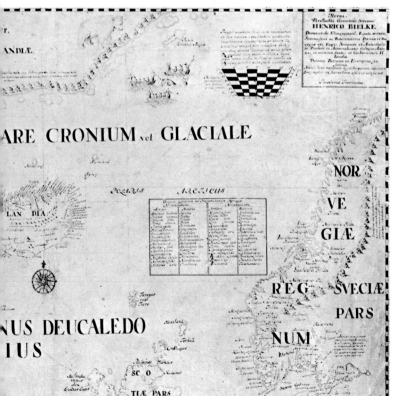

Greenland Rediscovered
- But the Maps Lie

Greenland was rediscovered–unintentionally–by an Englishman. In 1576, captain *Martin Frobisher* sailed from England to find the Northwest Passage to China. But first he found Greenland, which he thought to be Friesland–a mythical island which figured on the earliest maps. As a result, the southernmost point of Greenland was placed far to the north on Frobisher's maps. The disastrous consequence was that up until the 18th century the ships continued to hit the impenetrable, wind-swept and foggy ice masses of Eastern Greenland instead of sailing south of Greenland.

Frobisher's rediscovery of Greenland had no immediate significance for the Greenlanders. As proof of his discoveries, he brought home an Eskimo, but this man was caught at Baffin Island, not in Greenland.

The actual rediscovery of Greenland is attributable to captain *John Davis,* who was also an Englishman. Like Frobisher he tried to find the Northwest Passage to China and reached Greenland. Unlike Frobisher, however, he knew where he was. Davis was one of the most knowledgeable navigators of his time and during his three voyages to Greenland, from 1585-87, he charted the newly discovered areas. The Davis Strait is named in his honour.

He did not meet any Norsemen; they had disappeared forever, but he did chance upon some natives. One of his companions has told of this meeting which took place at what Davis called Gilbert Sound (a little north of the present Godthaab). "They (the Eskimos) made a lamentable noyse . . . with great outcryes and skreechings". John Davis ordered the ship's four-man orchestra ashore, and this caused much dancing on the rocks. The strangers did not, unfortunately, understand the natives' language. "Theyr articulation was very

hollow and throaty and theyr speech such that we could not understand it. However, we allured them by friendly embracings and signes of curtesie." One of them pointed at the sun and struck his breast so hard that we could actually hear the blow . . . Thereafter, I shook hands with one of them, and he kissed my hand and we won their confidence. We were in such high favour from this one meeting that we could have had everything they owned. We bought five kayaks and "theyr clothes from theyr backs. Everything was made from seal skin and birds' skin, theyr high boots, theyr breeches, theyr gloves–all of it carefully sewn and well tanned. We were wholly convinced that there were several artists among them."

Aside from a few episodes, caused by misunderstandings, the meeting passed off very peacefully. Typically for the English, a football match was arranged between the sailors and the Eskimos.

In Denmark there was a growing interest in the rediscovery of Greenland.

English rendering of Frobisher's fight with the Eskimos

In 1579, King Frederic II took the Englishman *James Alday* into his service. Two ships were sent off, they landed in the ice masses of East Greenland and barely managed to return to Denmark–but without results. Two years later Alday tried again, but made the same mistake of sailing north of Iceland.

Finally, in 1605, the first Danish

This is how the Northern Regions looked in the eyes of Adam of Bremen. Greenland has been reduced to a smaller island east of Iceland

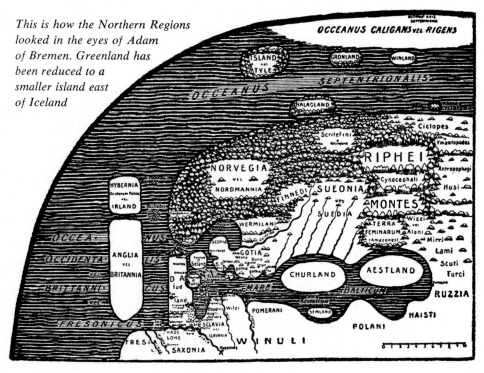

expedition, commanded by admiral *Godske Lindenow,* reached Western Greenland. They did not find any Norsemen, but they kidnapped some of the Greenlanders. Later on, the natives took a bloody revenge when they recognized one of the kidnappers, the English pilot, James Hall. In 1612 he sailed on his fourth voyage to Greenland, officially to find the Northwest Passage, but actually he was searching for valuable minerals. In the fjord where Godske Lindenow had taken the five Greenlanders prisoners, Hall was recognized as one of the kidnappers and killed.

But robberies and killings did not

So called land views, sketched by James Hall during his various voyages. From the top down: Cape Farewell, Cape Christian and Cape Desolation

stand in the way of peaceful dealings with the Greenlanders. They lacked iron tools and bartered with skins and narwhal tusks (believed to be the horn of a unicorn) which at one time brought up to 5000 dollars per tusk at the European royal courts.

And in high castles and low dives tales were told of the strange, far-away land with its rich fauna and squat natives who sailed their one-man boats which they could turn up-side down. Accounts of Greenland were published in many languages, often supported by imaginative sketches and engravings.

The original manuscript of the description of Greenland, written in 1067

The learned ADAM OF BREMEN, principal of the cathedral school in Bremen from 1067, was not too well-informed about Greenland. He wrote for instance: "Furthermore there are several islands in the great ocean, whereof Greenland is not the smallest, lying deeper out to sea in line with Suedia mountains, or the Riphesian ridges. To this island, it is said, you can sail from the Norman beaches in five or seven days, like to Iceland. The people there are blue-green from the saltwater, and from this the area has its name. They live in the same manner as the Icelanders, with the one exception that they are more cruel and alarm the seafarers by their violent attacks. It is also said that Christianity has flown to them." This is the oldest known account of Greenland.

"To Catch the Savages"

On July 28th 1605 a great crowd was gathering in Copenhagen, in fact the beach was black with people. Even the king, Christian IV, was present. The good ship RØDE LØFFUE, under command of Admiral Godske Lindenow, was about to put into port. The half-forgotten Greenland, which belonged to the crown, had been recovered, and as proof of this, the admiral had brought back two savages.

These had been caught at the present Fiskenæsset, south of Godthaab, and it had taken ten sailors and a big fight to overpower them on the coast. The Greenlanders went absolutely berserk when they came on board admiral Lindenow's ship. One of them grabbed a sword, but took hold of the wrong end and cut himself severely. Two weeks after admiral Lindenow's arrival, two other admirals, *Cunningham* and *Hall* commanding the ships TROST and MARE-KATTEN, arrived in Copenhagen also bringing back some Greenlanders. They had been as far north as Holsteinsborg where they went man hunting. This resulted in a big fight on the beach: "and they took 3 Greenlanders captive, with great danger of theyr lives, and they killed many of them."

But when the three arrived in Copenhagen, they understood how to take advantage of the situation. The Spanish ambassador gave them a big sum of money, and the three Greenlanders strutted about like squires with swords and hats with ostrich plumes, playing the role of "great gentlemen from Greenland". In 1606 they should have returned to Greenland–to help as interpreters and with the bartering. Five of the royal ships were leaving for Greenland, but two of the Greenlanders died on the way, and nothing is known of the fate of the last one.

The drama on the coast of Greenland repeated itself. The ship ØRNEN took five natives on board. One week later, one of them sprang overboard. The others came to Denmark. One day, two of them started up the Sound in their kayaks in an attempt to get home, one was caught but the other was out of reach and disappeared. The rest lived for almost 12 years in Denmark, where they died from grief and homesickness. During those years, the captains had a standing royal order to bring back a couple of young natives about 16 to 20 years old, who could be taught "piety, the Danish language and book learning". This turned out to be a rather difficult task, because the Greenlanders kept away from the ships. In one case, two had been caught and tied to the mast, but they jumped overboard later.

Half a century passed before any more Greenlanders came to Denmark. In 1654 a kidnapping took place in the Godthaab district during David Dannell's third voyage. While the Danes were trading with the natives, one of the women who had come aboard wanted to buy some knives from the boatswain. She offered him a skin from a seal, but this he thought too little. Then she offered him her own skin pants and started to remove them right on the deck. The boatswain motioned to her not to do that while other people were looking, and he induced her to go below deck together with her father, *Ihiob* and some other women. As soon as they had stepped below, the sailors battened down the hatches. These Greenlanders were first put ashore in Bergen, Norway, and here the girl's father thought that he could act like the Danes did when they came to Greenland. He put his hand on the thigh of a stately lady to have some fun with her. The father died, incidentally, before their arrival in Copenhagen. The girl and the two other women were sent from Copenhagen to the King who had taken up residence in Flensborg, because the capital was plague ridden. Here the women lived a very quiet life; they were treated well, but finally succumbed to the climate and the different way of life and died. They never became Christians even though they learned to speak Danish. When grace was said, they began to laugh.

It is easy to understand why the Europeans wanted to see the Greenlanders with their own eyes. The arctic voyagers had brought back imaginative descriptions of the natives; these, however, were not very accurate. Olaus Magnus' drawing from 1557, showing a Norseman's fight with a skrelling, who looks like a pygmy, is not very correct. Neither is the rock Hvitserk at right. It does not exist at all

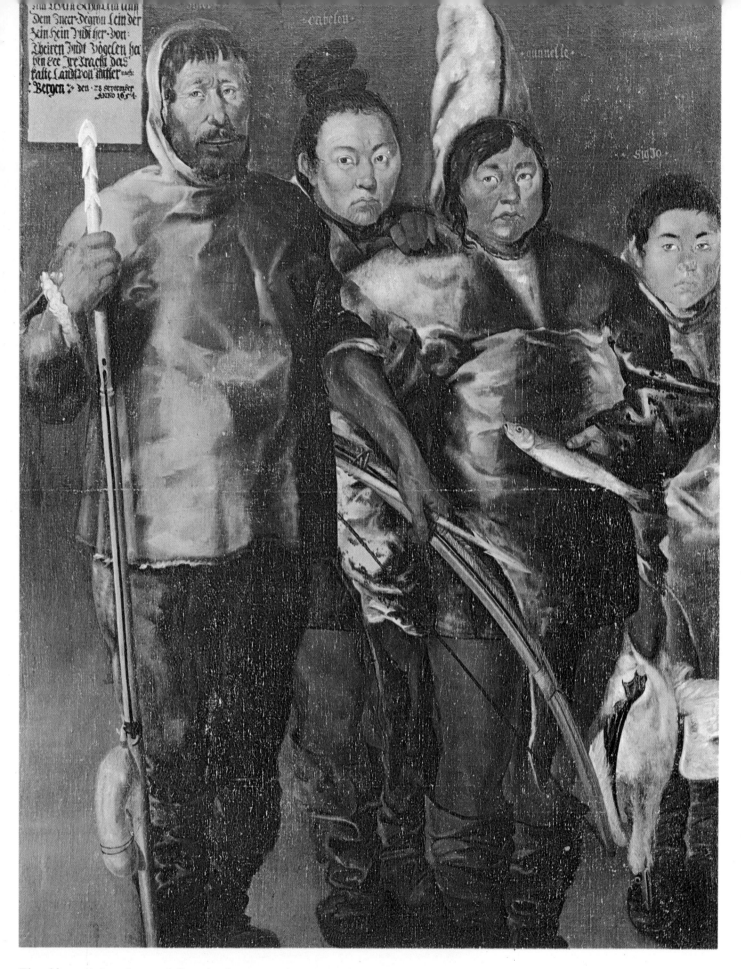

The oldest existing picture of Greenlanders, painted in Bergen by Salomon von Hauen. The picture now hangs at the National Museum in Copenhagen. The German inscription behind Ihiob reads: "In their small leather ships, the Greenlanders sail hither and thither on the ocean; from animals and birds they get their clothes. The cold land of Midnight. Bergen, September 28th, 1654."

Man of the World - With Kayak and Plumes

None of the Greenlanders who came to Denmark during the 17th century returned to their kinsmen, but the stories of how they were kidnapped lived on for more than one hundred years. When *Hans Egede,* the apostle of Greenland, arrived there in 1721, the people still knew the names of those who had been abducted seventy years before.

The next Greenlanders to visit Denmark came of their own free will. They were urged to leave by Hans Egede "for the Sake of Enlightening These poor People", so that they may receive "a fundamental Impression in Their Hearts of The True God's Knowledge".

It happened to be *Poek* and *Quiperoq,* who in 1724 ventured across the big ocean. They were received by King Frederic IV on his birthday where they displayed their kayaks on Esrom Lake and harpooned the royal ducks.

On November 9th, 1724 a Greenland pageant was held in Copenhagen with a sailing race–the Greenlanders' kayaks against the royal rowers. Poek and Qiperoq also displayed their duck hunting.

Qiperoq never returned to Greenland. He died in Bergen and had a beautiful funeral and a coffin with a name plate. Poek, however, returned in 1725 with three big chests filled with valuables.

He told the Greenlanders of the land of the bearded, where there were no mountains except the houses, and where some are rich and others have neither house nor clothes and have to beg from door to door. Apparently, he also visited the ale-houses. "There are many Houses where the Householder does nothing but sell Water which makes you quite mad. There they drink and yell and scream and fight and are without Reason."

His description of the country, abundant with tasty berries and fruits on the trees, lived on for more than one hundred years and has caused the

The stately painting of Poek and Qiperoq, hanging at the National Museum in Copenhagen

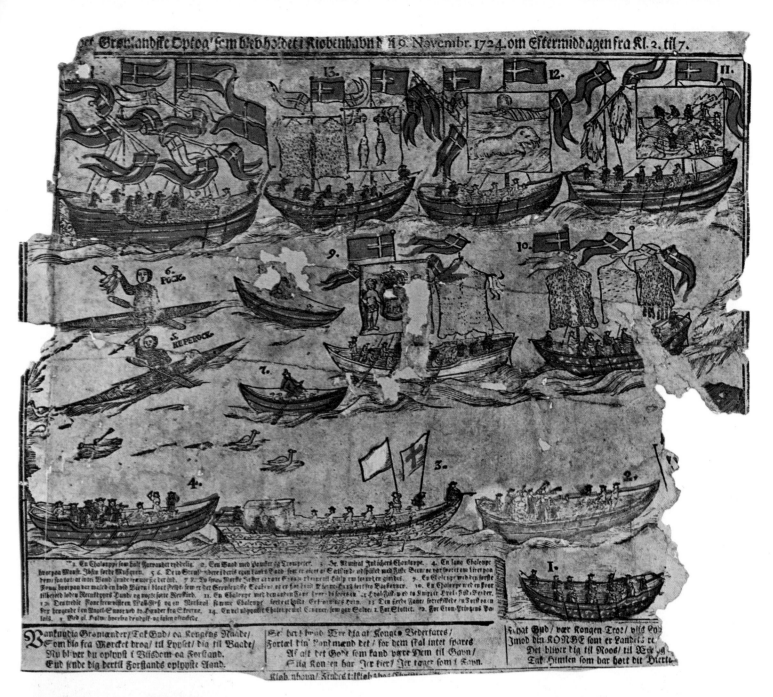

ber Grønlandske Optog/ som bleb holdet i Kiøbenhabn d. 9. Novembr. 1724. om Eftermiddagen fra Kl. 2. til 7.

Poek and his wife lived in Copenhagen's most fashionable circles. The text, written in the Greenland language, reads: "Poek and his wife are here seen in the presence of several church dignitaries, whose questions about the Greenlanders' attitude toward Christianity they are answering." Drawing by Aron

Greenlanders, right up to our times, to look upon Denmrak as the promised land.

In 1728, Poek returned to Copenhagen with some other Greenlanders, and now he had become a man of the world. He developed a taste for the songs and sounds of drinking. One Chrismas Eve he failed to return to his lodging house and did not appear until the next day–minus his hat, sword, snuffbox and scarf and looking "very downcast". Apparently he had fallen into bad company during his rounds of the city. Poek, his wife and the other Greenlanders died later from smallpox. Twelve students carried them to their graves.

The pageant on November 9th, 1724 in Copenhagen. The original–but somewhat damaged–woodcut is hand coloured. It is kept at the Chart and Picture Collection in the Royal Library in Copenhagen. The importance of the Greenlanders is clearly evident from their size in comparison with the rowers. Several of the royal barges carry pennants with motives from Greenland. No.12 has a narwhal and a walrus and number 9 has a polar bear on a blue background, the coat of arms of Greenland

33

How the Artists Imagined the Greenlanders

In early accounts the Greenlanders are described as well-proportioned, but with small hands and feet. An English account tells that "they have eyes like the Chinese, and if you wash them, their skin is of no darker colour than the skin of the Portuguese. Some of the younger girls have very beautiful eyes."

"In some tribes we saw natives with Roman noses, giving the person an air of dignity; but the majority had flat noses in their broad, almost circular faces. Their mouth is usually open and gives an impression of stupidity. They have a big mouth and their strong teeth are deeply rooted in the gums."

The writer ends up by telling that, admittedly, the Greenlanders are a strong people, but they cannot compare with the Europeans in athletic games.

The first Eskimo to arrive in London, here drawn by a Flemish artist. He is portrayed with all his harpoons, from which, apparently, he did not wish to part

34   *Various Eskimo types in an old German drawing. "If you wash them, they are of no darker colour in their skin than the Portuguese."*

At left in this old German drawing from "Missions Bilder" two Greenlanders with an almost European look are pictured. They are winning copper. The Eskimo at right is from Labrador and carries a child in one leg of her breeches

A formidable Eskimo with his family. From the Arni Magnússon Collection

A Dutch sailor's meeting with the Eskimos. The picture is from the handwritten "Enarrationum Historicarum de Gronlandia" by Matthiae Henrici Schachtii, 1688. From the Arni Magnússon Coll.

The Struggle for Oil
for the Lamps of Europe

In the wake of the many voyages of discovery followed an increasing interest in the arctic regions. Especially the Danes, the Dutch, the English and the French were competitors. In 1614, the Dutch started the Nordsee Compagnie which sent a shipmaster to Davis Strait and the West Coast. This was the beginning of a century-long struggle for whale oil for the lamps of Europe. Tens of thousands of Europeans came in closer contact with the legendary Eskimos.

The Danish king's reaction was to set up two Greenland Companies. However, in comparison to what the Dutch got out of their Greenland voyages and their trade with the natives, the Danish sailings showed very poor results. One thing emerged from this, though: the coat of arms of Greenland–a walking, and later on a sitting polar bear–was made part of the Danish national coat of arms, hereby emphasizing the Danish-Norwegian sovereignty over this distant land.

As a result of the trading situation all of the earliest detailed maps of Greenland were Dutch. The map at right is probably made in 1666 and is more accurate than any Danish map from the same period. As a matter of curiosity, it might be mentioned that for many years the Danish fleet sailed by Dutch charts–even long after the Danish charts had become more precise than the Dutch.

Whaling in East Greenland at the end of the 18th century. The picture is painted by an unknown artist and is kept at Altonaer Museum in Hamburg

An English artist's rendering of a dramatic situation at the West Coast of Greenland

Thanks to the whalers, the Dutch knew better than any other nation where Greenland was and how the coast looked. This chart from a Dutch atlas was probably drawn in 1666. As shown, the Dutch believed that the southern part of "Groen-Landt" consisted of two big and some smaller islands

37

The Bloody Century

The whaling period, a century-long drama of blubber, blood and genever, began around 1650. Germans, Norwegians, French, English, but in particular the Dutch, simply murdered the whales, and now and then the Greenlanders, too. At the cost of many lives, ten thousand men caught about 1000 great whales annually.

At that time Greenland really yielded a profit. Net profits for the Dutch were 1,351,000 guilder for the first decade and for the following decade nearly two million guilder.

Discipline was strict. The death penalty was introduced for murdering the Greenlanders. If a person shirked his duty, he was tied by the legs and dipped into the ocean from the main mast. Later he received three lashes with a rope end from the crew members. Anyone appearing unwashed at mealtimes had three lashes, too. Anyone using a knife against his fellowman had his right hand transfixed to the main mast with the same knife.

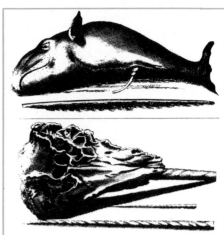

The unicorn, a legendary animal, was thoroughly described in the travel accounts of the day. These drawings of the unicorn, i.e. the narwhal and its peculiar tusk–originate from a book called "An Account of a Most Dangerous Voyage"

Dutch whalers near Greenland. The artist had never seen a polar bear –this might be the reason why it looks rather peculiar

During the whaling period, the definition of Greenland was not very clear. In 1624, Christian IV said: "By Greenland We understand all the lands north of Iceland and the North Cape."

People believed that Spitsbergen, which had been discovered in 1596, was part of Greenland, and that the arctic area was one land.

The Dutch took the liberty of forgetting that it was Denmark that had recovered Greenland after the Norse times; they moved about in the land as if it belonged to them. Dutch ships pushed their way northward to Upernavik, and numerous place names in Western Greenland are of Dutch origin.

Not until the year 1691 did the Danish "Absolute Monarch over Greenland" reflect on his inheritance and put an embargo on the Hanseatic sailings on "Our Streams for Greenland".

A flock of enraged walrusses attack a boat full of English sailors. Life at that time was harsh and the whalers were ruthless

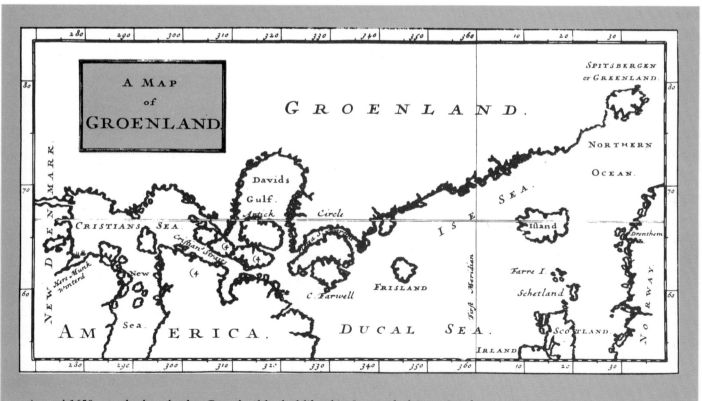

Around 1650, people thought that Greenland looked like this. It stretched from Spitsbergen to America

The Whales Hit Back

Most whaling voyages to Greenland began with a prayer: "God Almighty, immortal King, invisible and eternal, Creator and Saviour of Man." Nevertheless, He did not always protect the whalers. Thousands lost their lives in the arctic waters.

Their most dangerous opponents were the ice, scurvy and the whales. As a rule, the ice swallowed entire crews, while the scurvy hit at random. The deficient fare–salt pork, mouldy bread and soup –could not keep the scurvy away. It started with bleeding of the gums and then their teeth fell out one by one. The bleeding continued and only vitamin C could chase death away. But they did not know vitamins. The only thing they knew and wondered at, was the excellent health of the natives. The Greenlanders had strong teeth and did not suffer from scurvy. Not until late in the whaling period did the whalers think of letting their sick stay with "the savages" and live like them. As a rule, the sick became well again.

Whaling was in itself a deadly dangerous trade, and the whales hit back good and strong. They were attacked from small boats, but very often a whale turned against his attackers. Captain *William Scoresby*–the man who discovered and named the world's longest fjord, Scoresby Sound–tells how one of his harpooners was killed. "He had just flung his harpoon at a whale, when it hit him with a stroke af the tail. This one stroke broke all his ribs and practically all the bones in his body."

Captain Scoresby also tells of how a wounded whale attacked every single boat in the vicinity. It succeeded in making several of them capsize.

An episode from Labrador is illustrated here. The whale had been harpooned from two boats; it emerged under a third boat which was hurled fifteen feet up into the air.

This drawing from William Scoresby's "Account of the Arctic Regions" illustrates how dangerous whaling could be. The artist is James Waddel (1820)

Danish and Dutch whalers near Spitsbergen, which at that time was considered part of Greenland. The baby seals were killed with clubs, while lying on the ice. The exact same method, is, in fact, still used today. The picture is from 1803

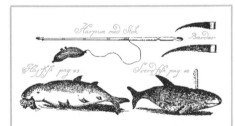

One of Hans Egede's numerous drawings of whales, from his "Perlustration". The Greenlanders' harpoon was different from the one the European whalers used

The English painter F. Willson has given several lively renderings of the whaling of the times. On one picture a whale is harpooned in the water, while the hunters on land are fighting a polar bear which looks more like a fabulous animal. On the other picture they are probably attacking a walrus

41

A Catastrophe in the History of Whaling

On June 24th, 1777, a vast whaling fleet rode at anchor off the East Coast of Greenland, close to the 75° lattitude, where the present Daneborg is. During the day it had been blowing up for a gale and thus one of the most dramatic chapters in the history of whaling began. Four days later 28 ships drifted into the field ice and became ice-bound.

During the following months some of the crews succeeded in getting their ships free, but twelve of them were stuck and drifted south with the ice. On August 19th, six of the ships were crushed in the pressure ice and sank only twelve nautical miles from shore.

At the beginning of October there was only one ship left and on the eleventh day this too was crushed. In the end, the ship had 286 survivors on board. The daily rations were reduced to ten tablespoons of porridge or pea soup. Some died from starvation, others froze to death and some drowned. Finally, the survivors decided to divide into groups.

One party marched to the north along the coast, another and bigger party decided to walk across the ice cap to the West Coast. None of them were ever heard of again. A third party of fifty men marched south and were rescued by Eskimos north of Cape Farewell.

A fourth party of well over 50 men chose to stay on the ice. They drifted around Cape Farewell and after incredible hardships and many deaths they reached Frederikshaab and Godthaab.

Six men who were on board their small boats when their ship was pressed down by the ice, rowed south rounding Cape Farewell. Late in the year they landed on a reef north of Godthaab, only half a nautical mile from the mainland. They did not know where they were, though, and decided to winter at the place. Using their sails and oars they built a hut. They were found at the end of March the following year by some Greenlanders who took them to Godthaab.

To avoid the ships being pressed down a channel was cut in the ice. Here two English crews are preparing to winter (1819)

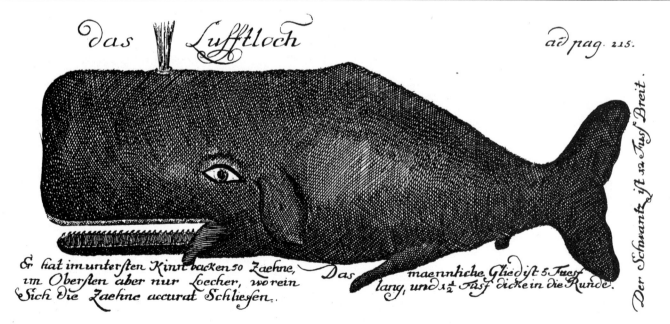

German drawing from 1738 shows a sperm whale which was found at Eydersted. It was 50 feet long and 12 feet high. The text tells that this enormous animal had 50 teeth in its lower jaw

Ordinarily, most of the shipwrecks took place in Melville Bay which was called Greenland's churchyard. In 1819 fourteen ships were shipwrecked in the ice, in 1821 eleven ships and in 1822 seven ships, but 1830 was the record year for arctic shipwrecks.

It all started on June 19th during a snow storm from south-southwest. The ice pressed the whaling fleet together. Suddenly an enormous ice floe toppled over and in less than fifteen minutes the nineteen ships were reduced to matchwood. One thousand men were standing on the ice, having, however, secured a supply of food–and aquavit. The latter probably explains why the whaling ship "Three Brothers" shortly after was followed to its wet grave by a thunderous cheer.

The crews organized a huge tent village and they lived on the ice until they were rescued by other whalers.

Among the rugged English and Scots whalers the year 1830 was later commemorated as the year when the whalers "took a vacation".

Everything is lost. The ship has been pressed down by the ice and the polar bears are searching the area for food

Christianity Comes to Greenland

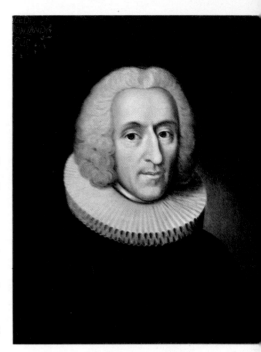

Even though Greenland belonged to Denmark, the Dutch were permitted to hunt and trade on the west coast for almost one hundred years without Danish interference.

But by and by the irritation grew in Denmark-Norway over the officious Dutchmen, and when at the same time a wave of pietism swept the Scandinavian countries, it was decided that something must be done.

On May 3rd, 1721 the small ship HÅBET sailed from Bergen with the double purpose of starting a trade with Greenland and, in addition, seeking the old Norsemen - who in all probability had forgotten their Christian faith. Two months later, at midnight on July 3rd, they cast anchor at a "seemingly good winter harbour".

The colonization of Greenland had begun.

Hans Egede, who was "head and chief" of the expedition, discovered, much to his regret, that the Norsemen were gone. Instead he started to convert the Greenlanders. It was difficult, however, to impress Christianity on "the savages", even though the text was paraphrased to read, "Give us this day our daily meat" instead of "Give us this day our daily bread", and "God's little lamb" was changed to "God's little seal", since the Greenlanders knew neither bread nor lamb.

As cross after cross was erected, the old necromancers were displaced little by little, but other than that nothing much happened. For 150 years the Greenlanders stayed at a very low stage of development, and not until 1850 did people in Denmark begin to criticize the miserable conditions under which the Greenlanders lived.

It took two world wars before anything decisive was done and a new life began for the Greenlanders.

To be sure, nothing but plastic flowers adorn the crosses on Greenland's churchyards, but the devotion to the faith, which the rigid, pietistic Hans Egede brought them two hundred and fifty years ago, is sincere enough.

Hans Egede Settles on the Isle of Hope

Hans Povelsön Egede, born in Northern Norway in 1686 and pastor in Vågan under the Bishop of Bergen, was convinced that the savages in Greenland were descendants of the Norsemen. For ten years he camped on the doorsteps of secular and church dignitaries, until in 1721, he was sent out as a missionary for money collected among the merchants of Bergen. For years he had felt "an inner Calling to preach the Gospel to the Heathens of Ice and Darkness". This calling gave rise to a big family row. His mother-in-law was furious and tried to influence her daughter, *Gertrud Rasch,* so that in the end "she regretted to have linked her fate with one who wanted to bring disaster on himself and his family". Fortunately for Egede, he quarrelled with his predecessor in Vågan, and both he and his wife took this as a Divine sign. She promised to follow him faitfully and this she did together with their four children.

The island on which they landed on July 3rd, 1721 was given the name "The Isle of Hope". It was a wind-swept place north of Godthaab Fjord where they hurriedly built the winter house which was to be their home for seven years.

His first meeting with the Greenlanders was a big disappointment to Hans Egede, and his first impression was such that he could do nothing but ask God to have mercy on them.

Two years later he tried to find the legendary Eastern Settlement and he succeeded in finding some Norse ruins in southern Greenland. He believed it to be the southern part of the Western Settlement, but in reality it was the Eastern Settlement he had found.

Hans Egede and his indefatigable wife, Gertrud Rasch, quickly won the Greenlanders' confidence. In order to learn their language he lived with them in their summer tent.

Those fifteen years constituted a

Hans Povelsön Egede, the Apostle of Greenland

never ending struggle to raise money to keep the mission going. When, finally, his appeal to the King was granted and the mission secured through a royal trading company, a new misfortune hit his work. One of the Greenlanders returning from Denmark was the bearer of smallpox which spread like lightning among the natives. At least 2-3000 people died. Of the 200 families in

Godthaabs Fjord hardly 30 were left. Hans Egede took this very greatly to heart and when his wife died from the strain of nursing the sick, he broke down completely. On August 9th, 1736 he left Greenland for good with her body. He did have the gratification, though, of seeing his son Poul continue his missionary work. In 1740 Hans Egede was appointed Bishop of Greenland.

Gertrud Rasch

Hans Egede's version of whales near Greenland

Hans Egede's map of Baal's Revier, the Isle of Hope, where he built his first winter house, and Godthaab where the first actual colony was founded

The front page of his famous "Perlustration"

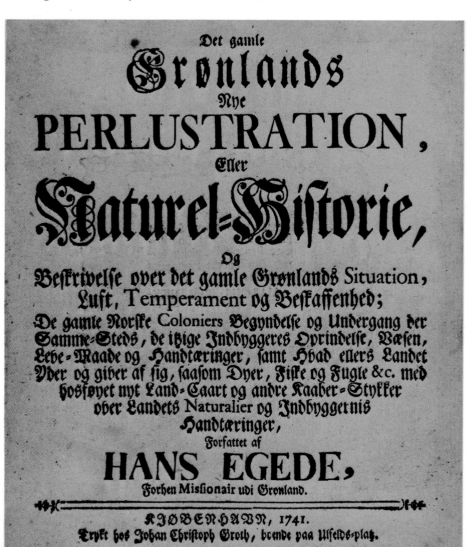

Det gamle
Grønlands
Nye
PERLUSTRATION,
Eller
Naturel-Historie,
Og
Beskrivelse over det gamle Grønlands Situation,
Luft, Temperament og Beskaffenhed;
De gamle Norske Coloniers Begyndelse og Undergang der
Samme-Steds, de itzige Indbyggeres Oprindelse, Væsen,
Leve-Maade og Handtæringer, samt Hvad ellers Landet
Yder og giver af sig, saasom Dyer, Fiske og Fugle &c. med
hosføyet nyt Land-Caart og andre Kaaber-Stykker
over Landets Naturalier og Indbyggernis
Handtæringer,
Forfattet af
HANS EGEDE,
Forhen Missionair udi Grønland.

KIØBENHAVN, 1741.
Trykt hos Johan Christoph Groth, boende paa Ulfelds-plaz.

Everyday Life in Greenland 250 Years ago

In "The new Perlustration from the old Greenland" *Hans Egede* described and illustrated the Greenlanders' daily life, as he saw it. When they go whaling, they dress as for a wedding–otherwise the whale will take flight, "because he likes not Un-cleanliness". About fifty people sail out in the umiak (the women's boat), and when the whale has been harpooned and killed with lances, they jump into the water, clad in waterproof sealskin. They cannot sink because the air inside the skins bears them up. Some dare-devils jump onto the back of the whale, yelling and screaming, even before it is dead.

One thing offended Hans Egede, of course–the Greenlanders' free and for them, very natural sexual habits. He writes that at first he thought that the men kept to their own wives, "but at long last we perceived that they are not terribly particular at that."

He describes how, after having eaten,

Hans Egede's account of a reindeer hunt. The women and children chase the reindeer along narrow paths and through mountain passes where the men are lying in wait

they start singing and dancing. "However, one after the other takes someone else's Woman behind a Curtain or Partition of Skin hung at one end of the House to the Bed, where they lay down and caress each other."

But, he goes on, no one but the married people attend these shameful adulterous games.

The women consider it good fortune and an honour to sleep with a necromancer or with one of their prophets or learned men. Many husbands gladly consent to it and go as far as paying them for sleeping with their wives.

The virgins and the young maidens, on the other hand, are chaste enough. Hans Egede adds that during the 15 years he spent in Greenland, he knew of only two or three girls who were in the family way without being married.

Hans Egede also recounts, how the Greenlanders do nothing but dance and sing all day and all night, when they have visitors. And, as they like to be praised for their virility and strength, they wrestle and play "hook" with their fingers and arms.

When the Greenlanders have visitors they do nothing but dance and sing all day and night, and as they like to be praised for their virility and strength, they wrestle and play "hook" with their fingers and arms

Hans Egede was an excellent observer and he has given detailed descriptions of the flora, fauna and of the people. He also found a remedy against the scurvy which at the beginning took such a heavy toll of lives among the colonists. "The lovely Cocleare Grass, which is the best Remedy against Scurvy, groweth everywhere in Greenland on the Ocean Side; it is not as bitter of Taste as the Kind growing with us, but its Use has very often, or so it is said, had miraculous Effects on the Sick. There groweth also a Grass with yellow Flowers, the Root of which smells as lovely as a Rose in Spring. The Greenlanders eat this Root and feel fine from it."

The Greenlanders are a stupid and callous people, he says, and so are their dogs. They are mute and do not bark, they only howl and whine.

Hans Egede also describes the marine life in text and drawings. He proves that earlier authors were mistaken about the unicorn. The correct name, he says, is the narwhal.

In the winter the seals are caught on the ice through the breathing holes. But in the spring when the animals are sunning themselves on the ice, the Greenlander camouflages himself with a seal skin and "crawls like a Seal towards them, nodding his Head up and down, purring and grumbling like the Seals do, until he gets so close to them that he can reach out with his Stick and thrust the Harpoon into them."

This lively drawing of Greenlanders going whaling is found in Hans Egede's Perlustration. In the background the three umiaks are hauling away an already dead whale

Seal hunting on the sea ice. The hunter sits in wait at the breathing holes or he sneaks up on the seal on shoes wrapped in bearskin. In the spring when the breathing holes are much larger, the hunters stand in a circle around the holes ready to harpoon the seals coming up for air
(Illustration from Hans Egede's book)

Hans Egede tells about the fauna in Greenland that he found wild rosemary with smell and taste like turpentine; when distilled it was used to make aquavit. There were birch trees as thick as a man's arm and angelica, tormentil, wild thyme, blueberries and crowberries

Hans Egede through Greenland Eyes

"And as Hans Egede rubbed the blind man's eyes with an ointment, he said that he (the blind) should believe in Jesus Christ for He was the only one who could restore his eyesight. Later, the Greenlander came up to the pastor and said that now he believed."
Ethnographic Museum, Oslo

"*The colony manager meets out punishment to the murderers of Samuel's brother-in-law*"–meanwhile Hans Egede is warning the natives not to kill each other
Ethnographic Museum, Oslo

"Hans Egede reprimanding a necromancer. Both Hans Egede and his wife seem to take the matter much to heart"

- and through Danish...

This picture of Hans Egede preaching to the Greenlanders was found in many Danish schools, right up to this century. He explained about the Devil: "The one called the Devil is not, like you think, the Souls of the Dead which can be seen. He is but a Spirit, which means that he is not Flesh and Blood, and very bad and Evil and designing to ruin People"

The Fight Against the Necromancers

Hans Egede's worst competitors were the necromancers, or angekokker as they were called. He says point blank that they are swindlers and liars, and that they work for the sake of lucre. They have made the poor gullible natives believe that they (the necromancers) can go straight to heaven even though they are tied hand and foot, and that they can also go down to hell, where the devil, Torngarsuk as they call him, lives.

Necromancy takes place in the homes at night. Angekokken lets himself tie up with a heavy rope, his head between his legs and his hands on his back–and a drum at his side. After the first song, the necromancer starts to yell and practice his sorcery, invoking Torngarsuk. Hans Egede claims that the necromancer knows how to change his voice. This way he keeps a running dialog, and all the while, he is getting rid of the restricting rope. He makes the audience believe that in less than no time he can fly through the roof and to the upper heavens where the souls of the most distinguished necromancers are assembled. Hans Egede adds, somewhat forgiving, that he does not believe that the necromancers really are the devil's disciples.

Among the Greenlanders Hans Egede was actually considered a necromancer. And to a certain extent he was himself to blame for this. There are several examples of how he, yielding to the natives' urgent pleas, tried to "blow on the sick". The rumours of his supernatural powers spread, particularly after some very successful cures. Once he was on a trip in Southern Greenland, when he washed a blind man's eyes with French aquavit.

Despite Hans Egede's missionary zeal, it took almost three years after his arrival before his first baptism took place. On January 24th 1724 he bap-

The Greenland tupilak, a helping spirit which can be enticed to kill others. You must be very careful with it, though, because if it returns it will kill you, too

tized a dying child. The father was a necromancer, who begged him to have the child baptized, because Hans Egede had said that otherwise it would not be saved. During the first seven years he did not baptize a single adult. Not only did he require religious knowledge, but he also wanted proof of their sincerity of faith and proof that their conversion had expressed itself in a prolonged change of life. This, in particular, proved to be a hard task, for, among other things, the Greenlanders had a difficult time understanding him.

Between times he had to use many Danish words. During the first few years he complained bitterly of the Greenlanders' callousness and their "innate Stupidity" and also that many who were "eager to hear the Word later got weary of listening, under the pretext of having heard it so often that now they knew Everything."

The first adult Greenlanders to be baptized were Poek and his wife, but they had already been to Copenhagen during the years 1724–25.

The adult Greenlanders did not let got that easily of the faith of their forefathers. The necromancers retained their hold on them and fought Hans Egede as a rival.

Avenging Themselves with Songs

Hans Egede is forever surprised by how peacefully and harmoniously the Greenlanders live with each other, "since Quarrels and Strifes, Hate and Covetousness you seldom notice in them." Disagreements occur, of course, but as a rule these are solved without shedding any blood. Hans Egede tells of how adept the Greenlanders are at composing satirical songs. The purpose is to outdo your opponent and make him look ridiculous. The song is supported by drumbeating, and when one party has finished his song, his opponent starts on his. The first one to run out of words, is the loser.

The Greenlanders were not always as peaceful as Hans Egede made them out to be. There are several stories, particularly of Dutch origin, of attacks and murders on the whalers. The Greenlanders had good teachers in the visitors who came to their shores during these years, especially the English who were known for their brutality. They robbed the Greenlanders of their catch, took the clothing off their backs, stole their boats and tackle and used the wood from their houses to burn on the ships. In 1728 people from Godthaab witnessed how two English shipmasters set fire to the Greenlanders' houses two miles out of town, "so that it looked like an unusually big fire". On the islands off the coast they collected eggs from the eiders, which they killed by the thousands.

Among the Greenlanders themselves both murders and blood feuds took place. The record was set by a man who had killed thirteen of his kinsmen.

Many stories of blood feuds and murders are found in the Greenland legends, here illustrated by Aron.

Egede describes in great detail how the Greenlanders spend their spare time. They love to play ball. This takes place when the moon is shining and they have two ways of playing. One is similar to handball and the other is actually foot-

Greenlanders playing handball and football

One of Aron's illustrations of a blood feud. A man returns home to find everyone murdered, among them his sister and her child. Then he takes a bloody vengeance by stabbing a pregnant woman with his spear

ball, where the purpose is to get as many goals as possible. But the games are actually of religious origin. "They tell me it is so, and also that the dead Souls play Ball in the Sky with the Head of a Walrus."

Hans Egede's description of a singing game in Greenland

"They eat Lice and Vermin"

Six to eight families lived in the native common houses. The house was heated by ten or twelve train-oil lamps which emitted such heat that "in the Winter it is as hot inside as in a Steam Bath, but the Air is not particularly good with them . . ."

Hans Egede could not stand this lack of cleanliness. He writes that they very seldom wash and that they eat from the same vessels and bowls that the dogs have eaten from, without cleaning them first. "They eat Lice and Vermin from themselves and others and it seems they scrupulously follow the old Saying that 'everything which comes from the Nose can fall into the Mouth', so that nothing will go to Waste. They scrape the Sweat off their Faces with a Knife and lick it up. They are not at all ashamed to relieve themselves in the Presence of others." Poor Hans Egede also had lice himself and suffered greatly from the vermin, because he lived like the Greenlanders and stayed with them in their own houses.

One evening, while Hans Egede lived with the Greenlanders, he had to vomit and then go to bed and pull his clothes over his face, because the rotten blubber and all the other filth "gave away such a Stench that it was unbearable."

Neither did he like the tattoos on the women. They tattooed themselves in the face and on their legs and thighs with a sewing needle and blackened thread. "It looks to me very ugly, but they claim it to be very amorous." They say, that if their face is not embroidered, their head will be turned into a train-oil lamp, when they get to heaven, or the land of the souls, as they call it.

He was rather irritated by the natives' use of amulets, beaks or claws, which they hung around their necks as protection against dangers and ill fortune. When he discovered this, he tore them off and threw them away, and if anyone objected, "they were given a Drubbing across their Backs."

He also threatened the obstinate with hell: "The Fire of Hell hurts very much and can never be extinguished. There, those who will not believe, will burn forever! The Flames will come out from their Eyes and Mouth, their Ears and Nose; The Devil will tear them apart with his Claws, and they will never be able to die."

And he tempted them with heaven: "Up there in the Heavens it is very beautiful; there we shall neither be cold nor hungry, we shall never get tired or grow old; there we shall live forever, there we shall always be happy, yes, shine like the Sun."

Godthaab
Founded by Convicts

Godthaab, the capital of Greenland, was founded by convicts. They came to the country seven years after Hans Egede and so terrorized his small congregation that for a while all his missionary work seemed to have been wasted.

The convicts were sent to Greenland at the order of the Danish king. He had attended to the matter of Greenland, since "Det Bergenske Companie" (the Bergen Company) which had sent out Hans Egede, had tired of the losing business. In 1726 one of the company's Greenland ships went down with all hands, and another ship arrived in Greenland so late in the year that it had to winter. After that the Norwegians had had enough of this experiment.

Hans Egede was heart-broken. In desperation he tried his hand at alchemy. Actually, this came very close to solving all his problems, because he and the members of his family almost died from the poisonous fumes from his chemical experiments. Then, finally, he was informed that the king had taken charge of the colonization. In 1728 five naval ships arrived in Greenland.

Onboard was Major *Claus Enevold Paars,* who had been named governor of Greenland and carried a royal order to ride across the ice cap and find the lost Norsemen. To this end he brought along horses, but the horses which did not die during the crossing, perished very quickly from hunger and cold.

Hans Egede had suggested to the king that the country be "colonized with Christian Persons", and to this end followed–aside from the soldiers and their wives–ten so-called prison slaves, convicts, and women from the House of Correction.

The whole gang was set ashore on the Isle of Hope. During the summer, however, the entire colony moved further up the fjord to Godthaab's present location, and soon debauchery started.

Godthaab around 1850. In the foreground, at right, Hans Egede's house

Fights and drinking were the order of the day. The Greenlanders were not only scared, they were also outraged. If *this* was part of the Gospel, they had no use for it and would be well satisfied with their own angakokker.

The soldiers were not very trustworthy either, and the officers had to take turns keeping watch at Hans Egede's house, because he was the one being blamed for bringing the Danish rabble to Greenland. In all probability, Hans Egede would have become Greenland's first–and only–martyr, had the colony not been attacked by scurvy.

Before the convicts and the thievish women of easy living were sent to Greenland, they were married at a mass wedding. General von Stöcken had orders to release ten slaves and marry them to the ten of the youngest, healthiest and strongest women, who in preparation for the wedding and their travels

to Greenland was to be given two suits and "the necessaries of food and keep." The selection was done by lot. One of the slaves was very lucky–he drew his girl's name. Her crime was that she, during a visit to Kronborg, where he was imprisoned on a minor charge, had exchanged clothes with him and had hidden herself in the cell, while he fled. He was caught shortly after and she was placed in the House of Correction. Hans Egede's son, Paul, writes about them: "They lived peacefully together and were the only ones to return of the whole lot."

King Frederic IV's historian expressed his indignation over the colonization problem in this way: "They let nothing but evil-doers marry by lot to equally many lecherous women and removed them to Greenland. It was very fortunate that most of them died from cold, hunger and scurvy."

Greenland's First Governor - A Thirsty Soul

The first governor of Greenland, Major *Claus Enevold Paars,* was an out- and -out bore. He was forever quarrelling with this men and their wives who, by the way, were a thoroughly bad lot. It made a very deep impression on the Greenlanders, when at one time two of the colonist women were flogged, respectively 50 and 27 lashes, just because they had cursed their husbands.

Paars and the commandant of the fort, whose name was *Landorph,* were jealous of each other. On one particular occasion, when they—as usual—had been drinking heavily, Landorph tore the wig off the governor's head, tramped on it; then he threw him on the bed and gave him a good thrashing. The subject of the controversy was the governor's mistress, Miss Anna Dorothea Titius, who wit-

nessed the punishment. She was in an advanced stage of pregnancy and very shortly after the incident gave birth to a daughter.

Paars has left a diary which reeks with self-righteousness. One place he writes in the most gushing language of how he let bring a pint of red wine to a very sick woman whose child of seven weeks had died in her arms, "even though she only asked for one glass."

With these notes Enevold Paars left himself a very sorry monument. When drawing the full picture of the man, it should be mentioned, however, that he tried to ascend the ice cap. He was not successful, though, but managed to drink a toast to the king on the spot— "an honour which has never of yore happened to this icy mountain."

Miniature portrait of Enevold Paars

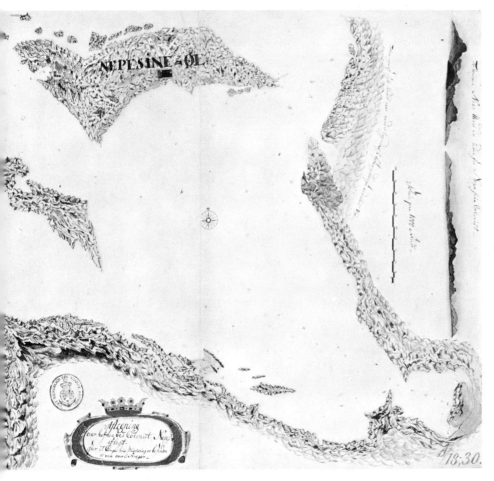

As part of the fight against the Dutch governor Paars, at the command of the king, built a fort on the island of Nepesine, north of Godthaab. Local disputes, in particular between Paars and the commandant of the island, led to a transfer of the troops to Godthaab. The year after, the Dutch set fire to the entire fort. The only thing left from this episode is this map from Hans Egede's times with the location of the fort

The First German Missionaries

Hans Egede had twelve years without competitors. Then came the first German missionaries from the Moravian Brethren, also called Herrnhuts. They were practical people who, aside from preaching and baptizing, also knew a profession. A short distance away from Hans Egede's colony, they build a, for Greenland, gigantic house. They called it Neu Herrnhut after the Moravian town, Herrnhut, in Silesia. The new missionaries were offended that their Danish colleague did not offer to house them when they arrived, and they started to build the day after their arrival. Hans Egede gave the excuse that he had not been requested to give them shelter.

In parallel rows next to the German mission stood some Greenlanders' houses and 12 winter houses, and a garden was laid out in the centre. The Moravian congregation had choirs divided according to age and sex; there were choirs of married men and choirs of bachelors, and there was the widows' assembly. Each choir had a special supervisor who should advise the individual choir members in religious matters. Aside from the Sunday services, the missionaries held daily evening meetings with songs and prayers, reading of the Scriptures and of devotional books. The assembly room itself could seat 300 people. The highest religious festival was Christmas. Everyone sang Christmas hymns throughout the night and early in the morning the congregation gathered in the assembly room which was lit by train-oil lamps out of sea shells. After the gifts from Germany were distributed the congregation walked to the Danish colony and woke up the people with music and song. This custom of waking people early on Christmas morning still exists.

The Moravian missionaries had a good grip in the Greenlanders. The services were very gay, and the missiona-

The Moravian missionary Mathias Stach once visited a family where an old woman had just died. Her children had already started to sew the shroud around her. The old woman was not quite dead, however; she started to moan and "Mathias Stach prevented their terrifying deed"

The relations between the missionaries and the population were not completely free of friction. The Greenland text tells us that at night when the missionaries slept in their tents, the Greenlanders came with their knives, but the missionaries chased them away

56

report from 1800 a Danish inspector suggested–after having toured Western Greenland–that the Moravian Brethren be ordered to leave the country.

But conditions grew worse and worse and in 1880 the bishops of the brotherhood decided to suspend their missionary work in Greenland.

The way in which these German missionaries met the population formed a glaring contrast to the goings-on in the Danish colony with the primitive and brutal whalers, drunken sailors and their strings of oaths. The German missionaries took care of the old and the sick, taught the Greenlanders to play the violin and the cither.

Neu Herrnhut as the mission looked the first 100 years. Painting by J. Aröe, 1846

ries had developed some rather subtle methods. This is evident, among other things, from some instructions specifically made for the purpose. "The Speaker must endeavour to arouse a sort of emotion in his listeners. And can it not be done in other ways, he must bring himself to cry, as especially some of the female sex easily let themselves move to cry with you."

The Moravian Brethren built a series of missions other places in Southern Greenland, always on the most idyllic spots with a view of the bluegreen ocean, icy mountains and snowy peaks. All this crowding together in missions caused the living conditions for the native population to fall below the subsistence level. They were hunters and in order to make a living they had to live spread out along the coast. And the missionaries could not offer any help; their own rations were very small indeed.

Even though the Danish authorities gave order to a spreading of the population, this order turned out to be practically impossible to carry out. In a

The mortality rate was fantastically high during the first mission years. The German missionaries worked very unselfishly and nursed the sick

The Hermit who Created the Greenland Written Language

Even though the Moravian Brethren as a whole might have had some harmful influence on the Greenlanders, they had at least one missionary who meant more to the natives than any other European. He was *Samuel Kleinschmidt,* son of the Moravian missionary in Frederiksdal. The boy was a linguistic genius and after having completed his education in Germany, he returned to Greenland in 1840 as the leader of the catechist school in Neu Herrnhut in Godthaab. He taught himself Danish and Latin in order to be able to work better with the Greenland language of which he had a most intimate knowledge. He was the founder of the Greenland written language.

Kleinschmidt was an eccentric. A Danish pastor, Carl Emil Janssen, who visited him in Lichtenfels in the year 1847 did not have one good word to say for him. He wrote about him: "They were all more or less scabious, in particular Mr. Kleinschmidt.

He looks approximately like this: with fiery red Hair and Beard, his right hand being especially scabious, was wrapped in a filthy Linen Rag, and because of this he held out his left in Greeting. On his Head he was bald, and the bare Spots were covered with Sores and Dirt. He does not use Underwear, and his Breeches had a big Hole in the Seat.

Samuel Kleinschmidt left the Moravian Brethren in 1859 and became a teacher at Godthaab Seminary. He translated textbooks and the Bible into the Greenland language and was instrumental in arousing the Greenlanders of the lethargy in which they found themselves at that time.

When Kleinschmidt left the Moravian Brethren, he built a small house with only one small room for himself. Here he set up his small printing press from which he published his own literary production. Kleinschmidt was a fantastically unassuming person. In the book, "The Art of Printing in Greenland and the Men behind it" the author, Knud Oldendow, says about the former Moravian missionary: "He hid his own personality very modestly behind the word "one". Once when a prince wanted to visit this strange man, so enveloped by myths, Samuel said, "One does not have the time" and slammed his door in the face of the prince. The University of Berlin wished to honour him with a doctor's degree for his famous grammar. Samuel answered with a refusal. "One does not use that sort of thing in Greenland"–and that was the end of that.

In his high age he was awarded the medal for meritorious services in gold, which he accepted but probably never wore. Once he said, "One does not wish any golden Medal on ones Anorak."

Samuel Kleinschmidt. Drawing from 1885

The mission of the Moravian Brethren in Frederiksdal in Southern Greenland

Habakuk and Maria Magdalene

Habakuk also held dancing festivals around the graves of the dead. Here he is dancing with members of the congregation. Watercolour by Kristoffer Kreutzmann

Hans Egede's Gospel in half Greenland and half Danish language, the pietism of the gentle Moravian Brethren, the tricks of the necromancers plus ancient Greenland hethenism was of course more than most Greenlanders could grasp.

In Evighedsfjorden near Sukkertoppen religion took a wrong turn. A revival started which spread to several parts of the coast of Southern Greenland. The originator was a baptized Greenlander, whose name was Habakuk, and his wife, Maria Magdalene. Habakuk was a rogue who had amorous affairs with a nice looking housemaid. But his wife was equally resourceful. Instead of making a domestic scene, she claimed that a long since dead couple had sought her out and revealed to her what Habakuk was doing. Furthermore, she had been told similar things about other people. She wrote down her "revelations" to the local pastor, Niels Hveyssel. He took the whole matter very sensibly and admonished Habakuk to be faithful to his wife, and then, he figured, Maria Magdalene would suspend her work as a profet.

But either Habakuk did not keep away from the girl or Maria Magdalene had found out that she had great influence in the settlement. At any rate, she continued her exposures, despite renewed warnings from the pastor. And at Christmas time 1788 the storm broke. One Greenlander claimed that he had heard the sounds of song and instruments in the air and had seen a great crowd of dead souls float in the air at a short distance from the earth.

Maria Magdalene immediately took the matter in hand and declared that she had had secret talks with the dead and that doomsday was near.

During the spring this romantic movement spread all over the district, and at the traditional reindeer hunts further inland, Maria posed as a prophet and leader of a new congregation. She held services with hymn singing, wild roars of laughter and kissing orgies.

This was just the thing for Habakuk. He appointed himself the great prophet. And when one of his wives became pregnant, he declared that she had been fecundated by the Holy Spirit and that she would give birth to a new Christ.

Unfortunately the baby was a girl.

Habakuk took pleasure in interrogating the congregation. The men stood in a ring about him, and with his eyes closed, Habakuk pointed out those with whom God was well pleased. The women, on the other hand, were placed on the bed next to each other. Habakuk stuck his head out from behind a curtain, selected the most beatiful, one by one. Those he "cleansed" behind the curtain.

By and by Maria Magdalene introduced very strict church discipline and at her own sweet will sentenced the members of the congregation to deportation, punishment or to death.

In the Greenland legends there is a description of such a religious killing. The poor woman, whom Habakuk and Magdalene had sentenced to death, was fetched in her tent. She was quite calm and took a pinch of snuff before they carried her out to a cliff. "And when they took her by the throat and were about to throw her into the Water, Habakuk sent Word to them and told them, that when they threw her out they should say nothing but: 'You pray for our Sins.'

Finally the case was taken up in Copenhagen where the clergy discussed it. It was decided that "the hag" should be put of the way "in whatever manner possible". However, it turned out that this was not necessary, because Habakuk was not able to resist temptation. Because of his "inordinate holiness" Maria Magdalene had rechristened him Jesus and appointed him father confessor for the women of the congregation. This, however, developed very quickly into nothing but promiscuity and from then on the movement disintegrated.

But the memory of Habakuk still lives on in Greenland.

59

The Trade Struggle Begins

"If you show a Greenlander a gold piece and a sewing needle, he will reach out for the latter. They cannot count to more than 21. They know nothing of what has happened before their own time. Yes, they do not even know how to tell their own age, since they know of no other calendar than the moon."

So declared the Mayor of Hamburg, Johann Anderson some time during the 1740's, and this was good to know if you were going to trade with the Greenlanders.

The Dutch had long since found out that tradings with "the savages" went more smoothly when they had been given sweet liqueur or genever. In return for shirts of the cheapest kind, stockings, mittens, tin kettles, knives, awls, fishing hooks, glass pearls and other catchpenny goods the Dutch got seal and whale blubber, whalebones, unicorn horns (narwhal tusks) and skins of reindeer, fox and seal. Two sealskins for one shirt!

And when the bartering was done, there was dancing on deck while down below the crew made merry with the Greenlanders' wives. No wonder that half of the population of Holsteinsborg to-day is said to be of Dutch origin.

But relations were not always that peaceful. Fights, killings and kidnapping of natives, who were displayed in Europe as rare animals, were part of the clash of the two cultures. The accusations of robbery, theft and murder were mutual. In 1720, the year before Hans Egede's arrival, Dutch shipmasters were accused of robbery, assault and murder, and strict punishment was introduced: "Any seafarer, who molests, attacks or steals the property of the natives, will at first lose his wages and afterwards, in proportion to his misdeeds, he will be punished as a pirate and public assaulter."

This did not do the Greenlanders much good, however, because it was a long way to the Hague and the provisions seemed more in consideration of the barter trade than of the natives. If a Dutch ship was shipwrecked or stranded, the Greenlanders, on the other hand, would murder the shipwrecked sailors.

The lawlessness lasted until long after Christianity, introduced by Hans Egede, came to Greenland. The Dutch did as they pleased. It is true that as early as 1636 a Greenland Trade Company had

The Europeans taught the Greenlanders how to steal. Theft was unknown in the original Greenland communities, where everyone depended on each other. The Greenland text reads: "Tusilartok's son, Aqajarok Ivsussog, with another Greenlander, has been locked in the cabin, because they have stolen some cheap trifles on board; but they broke down the door and sought safety in flight."

This is how they bartered in the first colonies. The Greenlanders are having their blubber weighed and get various European goods instead. A bookkeeper is carefully writing everything down

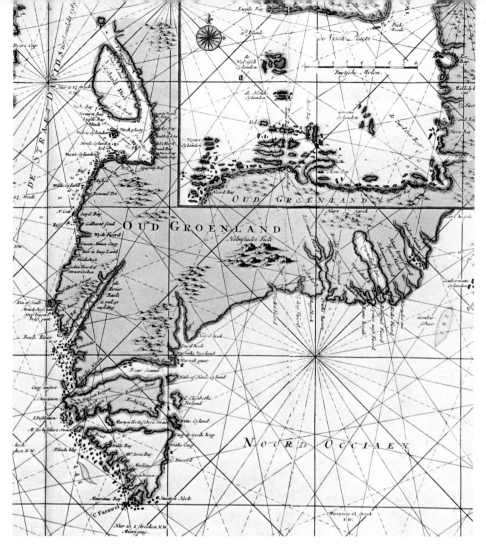

been established in Copenhagen, but the contact with Greenland was rather sporadic and the company was dissolved. In reality Hans Egede now had a trade monopoly through a trade company established in Bergen for the purpose of securing means for the continuation of the mission in Greenland.

But Hans Egedes "company" had even less success than his missionary works. Each year the Dutch sent 70 ships into the Davis Strait. The bartering took place in particular at the island of Nipisat south of Holsteinsborg, which had the best whaling grounds in the country.

Hans Egede's trading company was dissolved as early as 1726. After this the Danish government suggested to the Copenhagen merchants that they take over the trade, and in 1734 *Jakob Sewerin* was awarded a trade monopoly in return for an annual grant of 2000 rix-dollar to the mission.

Jakob Sewerin was the son of a town judge from Jutland, but at the age of 22 he had married a wealthy 62-year old wi-

dow from Copenhagen. Thus he became a merchant of note, specializing in trade with Iceland and the Finmark. He presided autocratically over the trade from his estate in Jutland. On several occasions he complained to the Danish king of the Dutch who ran away with his profit and finally a royal embargo was issued, forbidding the Dutch to touch at port in Greenland, except in case of emergency. Their trade with the natives was banned inside a five mile limit off the shore and they were not to sail any further north than Christianshaab.

One Dutch shipmaster, Jan Jobs, did not care two hoots about the embargo, but at Christianshaab he was seized by Sewerin's ships and his cargo of wooden boards was used to repair the houses in the colony. The year after, the Dutch turned up with five armoured vessels and declaired boastfully that it would cost plenty of blood if the Danes accosted them.

The flotilla put into Jakobshavn, and the chief refused to leave the harbour. Three of Sewerin's ships, including an armoured galeon, anchored outside the harbour. At midnight they opened fire and following a good hour's cannonade the Dutch surrendered.

The first "sea battle" to take place north of the arctic circle ended rather peacefully. The Dutch were brought ashore and started tackling the genever instead of the Danes. In the early morning of June 6th, 1739 the rocks echoed with yelling and singing. The place was then called Maklykout, and two years later a so-called mission lodge was established here with Poul Egede as the missionary. It was then named Jakobshavn after Jakob Sewerin. At first it was a trading station, then a whaling station and finally it was raised to a colony and the center of trade with the Greenlanders who lived further north.

The Danish State Takes Charge of Greenland

Little by little Jacob Sewerin's monopoly resulted in losses, and in 1750 the trade on Greenland was taken over by another private trading company which did not do any better, despite heavy government subsidies. The company was dissolved in 1774 and once more the government had to step in. By a royal decree of March 8, 1776 it was made official that the state had taken charge of all monopoly trade and that the country was closed for private trade. This state of affairs came to last 176 years.

During the first years the company had the very grandiose name "The Royal Greenland, Iceland, Finmark and Faroe Trading Company". Later, when the monopolies on Iceland and the Faroe Islands ceased, the name was changed to "The Royal Greenland Trading Company".

When the state took charge of the private company, this had an annual loss of 107,000 rix-dollar. The state trading had a very noble aim, namely "to the greatest extend possible safeguarding the interests of the natives"; but it would do no harm if it showed a profit too. And this it did for long periods. The profit varied from year to year, but as an example, from 1829 to 1850 it amounted to one million D. kr. annually.

The economic basis during the first one hundred years was the whale catch, which took place in particular around Godhavn and Holsteinsborg. In certain periods, 2200 barrels of train-oil were sent back to Denmark annually plus 18,000 pieces of whalebone.

One single whale gave from 200 to 250 barrels of train-oil, worth up to 60 pound Sterling per ton.

The whale bones had many possible applications. Among other things, they were used as "fishbones" (stays) in corsets.

The berth of the Royal Greenland Trading Company in Copenhagen. The picture painted by N. I. Bredal, is from 1810, but the big warehouses are still standing and still in use

64 Pounds of Gun Powder to Salute the Inspector

The royal state trading with Greenland was conducted from Copenhagen. This was very well known by any Copenhagener in those days, because the burning of the blubber sent an insufferable stench out over the entire city.

The trading company was an old venerable enterprise. The management consisted of four directors, who decidedly belonged to the older generation. At one time the management included one 80-year old, one 81-year old, one 61-year old; the youngest was 50 years old.

The two principal managers of the trade in Greenland were the inspectors for Northern and Southern Greenland, with residence respectively in Godhavn and Godthaab. It was the duty of the inspectors to make tours of inspection in their enormous district. As a rule this took place from an umiak. The inspector was a distinguished gentleman, who was received in style, of course. From an account from 1829 it is evident that 64 pounds of gun powder was used that year to salute Inspector *Fasting*. On the other hand, he used in gratuities 240 quarts of corn spirits, 170 quarts of malt and 4 pounds of hops for beer for the Greenlanders on the king's birthday, at Christmas and for the whale flensing.

The inspector was both chief of police and judge. However, if the punishment exceeded 15 lashes with the rope or a fine of ten rix-dollar, the accused could appeal to the management.

The individual colonies were managed by a colony manager who was also the shopkeeper. Under him served several assistants, the policemen, the foremen and other personnel.

Inspector Fasting did not mince his words when he described the personnel. He said outright that they had only come to Greenland, because they could not make the grade anywhere else. "Furthermore most of these who do service in this country, are often people who, because of intemperance or other faults, seem unable to earn a living at home. That such persons are unable to have any good effect, but in the contrary by their own example have a very harmful effect on the Greenlanders, ought to be obvious . . ."

But the management in Copenhagen was of the opinion that "the people rather often improved after having arrived in Greenland, where the access to aquavit is rather limited."

The highest state officials had handsome uniforms as a mark of their position. C. P. Holbøll was inspector for 28 years from 1828

This Greenland rendering of a Danish official is very much to the point. He travelled in style, swallow-tailed flag, long pipe and silk hat

Immorality and Depravity

The directors kept a sharp eye on the crews' relations with the Greenland women. This assembly of old men had decided that no one could marry without their permission. Police sergeants could get permission to marry European women or women of mixed blood. Junior policemen, however, could only marry women of mixed blood, but then they had to commit themselves not to leave Greenland. The directors thought this to be a practical arrangement, since permission was only given to the people they wanted to keep. But the aging directors were unable to restrain the hormones from a distance of more than 2500 miles.

The missionaries complained about immorality and depravity. To this the directors answered, "The Basis for this Evil is inherent in the Natives themselves.–These Children of Nature do not consider Moral Laxity a Vice and consequently they do not associate any Feeling of Shame with it, as does any cultivated Nation. They simply follow their animal Lust without the least Shyness . . ."

As a rule, children of mixed marriages were very unfortunate. They did not know the Greenlanders' ways of hunting or fishing and neither were they taught by the Danes. The authorities ,however, felt a moral obligation towards them. It was acknowledged, on the other hand, that many capable people were óf mixed blood. Their names recur in the present Greenland communities, particularly in

The Greenland women in particular were accused of laziness by the officials. In this steel engraving by A. Gusmand they look as if they are busily engaged with their tasks

some of the more well-known Greenland families living on the west coast.

In some narratives the Greenland women get a rather poor testimonial. One of the Danish inspectors maintained that the only thing the young girls learn is sewing. According to tradition the women must take care of the men's catch and their skins, "but as the Women partly from Habit, partly from Nature are very lazy, they generally undertake only the most Necessary of Tasks, and it is no rare Thing for many of the Skins of the Seals which the Men have caught, to rot away simply because the Women are too ease-loving to fix them. Love of Coffee and Gossip, Laziness and Filthiness are the predominant Traits of the Greenland Women."

The inspector suggested that they get better schooling and he wanted to establish a teacher's post at the Seminary in Jakobshavn. The directors, however, did not wish to recognize his critisism of the women. It was found too narrow -minded. Unfortunately, no reports from the Greenlanders to the directors, giving their views of the Danes, are known.

Even though the people were ordinarily kept on short commons, they still had their celebrations, particularly on the king's birthday. Shooting matches were held between the minor officials and the best hunters from the district. In the picture a fiddler is playing a tune while the gentleman in the centre, probably the inspector, is giving orders. The picture is painted by Aron

A Happy People - Polygamous from Inclination

The strange people who lived so far north that it seemed beyond reason, gave rise to numerous accounts in European books and newspapers. To be sure, the Copenhageners had seen a few of these savages during the 17th century, but far into the following centuries fantasy and not reality dominated in everything put into print about the Greenlanders. One German account describes the Greenlanders as being grayish, almost white in their skin. The difference in shades are caused by the various degrees of cleanliness.

At the close of the 17th century Sir *William Parry,* leader of several expeditionary forces, devoted some time describing the character traits of the Greenlanders. Earlier, he writes, they have been painted as either good or bad, but a description of their numerous virtues would make many a Christian blush with shame. Some have described them as the most barbaric and vicious people on earth. But they are neither repulsive, nor wild nor barbaric. On the contrary, they are a gentle, quiet and good natured race.

They live in natural freedom with no sort of government and have realized the modern republican's dream of a free society. You never hear them curse, scold or use obscene language, except for some nicknames which they use to describe a ridiculous situation. Neither boasting nor roars of laughter occur among them. Violent robberies do not happen either.

In continuing his general description of the Greenlanders' virtues, Parry also mentions the exceptions, like murders of foreigners and murders among the Greenlanders–usually an arrow or harpoon in the back–and blood feuds which often continue through several generations.

William Parry is not completely without criticism, however. He writes that you cannot always depend on the outward modesty of the Greenlanders and about their sexual habits he says with proper English disdain: "Polygamy is not always practised from a wish to beget offspring, but from sheer lust. Their women are just as clever at the language of the eyes as are the Turkish courtesans."

A perfect Greenland idyl around 1860. Summer settlement in a quiet fjord. Painted by Carl Rasmussen

A Brush Was Included with the Meals

The first Danish colonists in Greenland lived in such poverty as is hard to imagine.

In 1748 a Danish missionary complained that his mission room in Jacobshavn did not even have the space for a bed, a table, a pair of chairs and his chest. He did not even have a stove. In 1755 another Danish missionary from Frederikshaab complained of "this damp and musty room which is pinched and uncomfortable as well, with which I was nevertheless satisfied, inasmuch as it was not very near these coarse and incompetent people (the crew)." The vicarage in Godthaab had only two very small rooms at one end of the church. In 1767 the chapel in Holsteinsborg was so leaky that is was impossible to "lie dry in the beds" and books and furniture were ruined by water. In 1795 the pastor's room in Umanak was still so leaky that the snow sweept about his ears while he was writing his sermon. The walls in the half-timbered house were so thin that the room could not be properly heated even when using plenty of coal.

The voyage to Greenland sometimes took almost four months, if conditions were particularly bad, but in any case it lasted so long that the serving of fresh food was impossible. Peas and grain were very often mouldy, or spoiled by mice. It also happened that the bread "was so full of spiders and webs inside that one always had to have a feather wing ready" when eating.

Once having reached Greenland, conditions were no better. In 1831 inspector *W. M. Olrik* wrote in "Köbenhavnerposten" (a Copenhagen newspaper) that the year 1812 "in more ways than one was a remarkable year. Thus, any proper Meal included a Brush to brush off all the Mouldiness from the Hardtacks. The Inspector was the Inventor of this Device; it was soon rejected, however, because this Brushing took up too much Time for empty Stomachs and brought about a constant Sneezing, wherefore the Hardtacks were called Sneezing Bread."

The missionaries and their people sufered the most, and oftentimes they complained that the colony managers treated them unfairly. But each year saw a time of fasting which just hit everyone. Even coffee, tea and sugar was in short supply. They had a proverb which was used at the end of the year: "Come Christmas, come Christmas, come Falalala, come Easter, come Easter, God will help me then."

At one point, joint housekeeping for the colony managers and the missionaries was tried out, but this caused such dissension that the arrangement was soon abandoned.

The "Eating Regulations of May 23rd, 1771," according to which the standing crews serving in the Royal Authorized General Trading Company were fed, read in part: Monday, Friday and Saturday Porridge morning, noon and night. On Tuesdays, Wednesdays and Thursdays porridge in the morning and pea soup at noon and in the evening. On Thursdays meat with the evening pea soup. On Sunday pork and pea soup at noon and only pea soup in the evening. This day the morning meal consisted solely of aquavit.

In general the relations between the Danes and the Greenlanders were good. Time and again the willingness of the

Fiskenæsset (the Fishing Cape) was established in 1754 as a trading station in order to make travelling easier between the two colonies Godthaab and Frederikshaab

population to "obey given orders", their helpfulness and kindness is being stressed. It is an exception when it is reported that the official sloops in Godthaab were sometimes stolen by the Greenlanders, who sailed out to the English whalers and came back stone drunk.

They could not be punished for this. An admonitory speech was made in the presence of the missionary–so that the Greenlanders would understand that God was on the side of the trading company.

Upernavik was the exception to the rule about peaceable relations with the Danes. The population here was composed of a good many heathens, and even though many of them had been baptized, the missionaries had only succeeded in giving them a thin veneer of Christianity. The local necromancer had much more power over the people. In the reports are told of several killings. For instance, two old men had been murdered and afterwards, with the necromancer in charge, the Greenlanders planned to kill the colony manager and the other Danes in the colony. Killings of children took place, too. A ten-year old boy who suffered from convulsions was buried alive, naked and tied hand and foot.

The colony in Upernavik was established in 1772 and the officials consisted of the colony manager, his assistant, a cooper, a carpenter, the colony and mission cook plus four sailors. During the first few years of the colony five colony managers died. The same applied to the assistants, and most of the others left the colony crippled. Several committed suicide, among them an old assistant who tied himself to a seal net and jumped through a breathing hole in the ice. In 1787 a surgeon was hired as an assistant. He died before the end of the year, even though he was in excellent health.

The reason was–as in all the other cases–scurvy. Finally, the missionary was the only official in the colony and he was later rewarded by the directors of the trading company with "a pair of silver table candlesticks".

The exact population figure was not known, but statistics from 1834 give the total population as 7552. The trading company was, of course, very interested in an increase, because then the profit would rise.

Inspector Holböll in Southern Greenland writes in one of his reports that the male Greenlanders, particularly in the Julianehaab district, married rather late and very often with older women. The young people often lead a disorderly life and therefore became second-rate hunters and fishermen. In order to increase the population, the inspector arranged that each Greenlander under the age of 24 was given a rifle if he married a girl of no more than 20. The population figure rose almost at once. In 1855 it was 10,000.

The kayak mail has been taken on board an umiak

MAIL BY KAYAK

The colonies very seldom had contact with each other, but once in a while urgent letters were sent from one colony to the other. This was done by kayak mail. Bringing the mail from Julianehaab to Frederikshaab, for example, was paid with 12 pounds of bread and 10 rix-dollars, while a trip to Sukkertoppen from Holsteinsborg earned 4 pounds of bread, half a pint of aquavit and half a pound of English tobacco plus 8 rix-dollars. A regulation from 1873 had it that "Regular Mail is sent three Times a Year: in the Winter or the Spring, in the Summer, and in the Fall, the Inspectors deciding the Hours of Departure and Collection." The mail was transported free of charge. Parcel post and stamps were not introduced until 1905.

The Sea Route - a Thread of Life

The sea route to Greenland was the thin lifeline which connected the colonies with the motherland. Without this, the people did not have sufficient means of existence. Time and again the so-called "starvation diet" had to be distributed among the Greenlanders when the hunting failed. If the ships carrying provisions or equipment failed to arrive, the situation was almost disastrous.

And many ships never made it. Just as Eric the Red's immigrants had discovered, the waters around Greenland are some of the most dangerous in the world. The ice has caused numerous shipwrecks, and no castaway could survive in the icy cold water for more than 5-10 minutes.

Often as not the ships used were rather small, pinks, hookers, ketches, brigs and a few barks and frigates. Their size varied from 45 to 400 tons. During the time of the old sailing ships a voyage to Greenland often lasted several months. There is an example of a journey from Copenhagen to Julianehaab taking 245 days.

Aside from storm and ice the worst enemy of the ships was the scurvy which raged among the crews during the month-long voyages when they had nothing to eat except hardtacks and salt pork. The weekly ration per sailor consisted of 1½ pounds of salt pork, one pound of smoked meat, one pound of butter, five loaves of bread plus peas, grain and ale. But what meat and what butter? After several months of sailing it was uneatable.

When there were survivors from a shipwreck, a maritime inquiry had to be held. If the accident happened in the Davis Strait, then it was the job of the inspector, even though he lacked maritime knowledge. When the ship GERTRUD CATHRINE was shipwrecked after having collided with an iceberg on a trip from Godhavn to Claushavn, an inquiry was held. From this it appeared that apart from the boatswain, "some were second-rate sailors and the rest were very inexperienced, indeed."

During the above inquiry, interest centered on the fact that a red checked featherbed, belonging to the missionary's wife, Mrs. Cappeln, a small pig and one cask of aquavit had been saved. On the other hand, there were several conflicting explanations as to the whereabouts of a blue striped featherbed belonging to the colony manager.

The records of the court tell of one shipwreck after another. Some of the sailors were saved but many perished. The fate of the frigate MARIA LOVISA is just one example of how ghastly some of these voyages to Greenland were:

Maria Lovisa weighs anchor from Copenhagen on June 14th, 1800. Near Elsinor she is wind-bound until June 21th. On June 22nd Norway is in sight. On June 30th she rides out a gale at Lindesnæs. Here one of the sailors, Jacob Larsen, dies from scurvy. On July 7th the ship is off Fair Isle in a new storm. The crew is soaking wet. On August 23rd Jens Nielsen, an able-bodied seaman, is relieved from his duties because of scurvy. On september 6th, the seamen Jacob Torpegaard, Hans Hansen and Jørgen Rasmussen have to be relieved from their duties because of scurvy and rheumatism. On September 14th the captain, who is so weak he cannot write, is asking his first officer to take command. On September 19th second officer Theisen dies from scurvy. The captain dies on September 21st. Finally, on September 28th the ship is within sight of land, but fog and snow prevent them from making a landfall. On October 1st two Greenlanders are taken aboard. That night one more sailor dies. On October 4th the ship is helplessly drifting north. No one is able to reef the sails. On October 11th

The whaling brig FREDERIKKE LOUISE. *Painting by E. A. Petersen*

another storm. On the 12th land is again within sight and they drop anchor. They were in the Ameralik fjord near Godthaab. Three men, still able to row, are being sent ashore to find some Greenlanders. They return to the ship on the 15th completely exhausted. On October 23rd they weigh anchor again, but meet with a storm which carries the ship against the rocks. Here she heels over to port and the wheel breaks.. All masts are cut away to right the ship. They fail to save her. The boats are lowered, and the rest of the crew, in a most pitiable state, row into Godthaab.

Tale of an "Embarker"

From the point of view of the passengers–the so-called "embarkers"–the voyages to Greenland could hardly be called luxury trips. The following is an account of such a trip made in 1863 by a junior officer, *Eduard Thomsen* on board he brig TJALFE. He was given a small room in the aft hold, sharing it with another officer. It was 5 feet long, eight feet wide and separated from the rest of the hold by just a few stinking boards. The entrance to the "cabin", which he dubbed he "Lobster-pot", was the aft hatchway which was closed as soon as they had gone down. The cabin had no room for bunks so they slept on the floor. "I shall not soon forget how uncomfortable it was, and that no Attempts whatsoever were made to change this. I would never have offered even the most miserable of Beggars suchlike Quarters for a single Day."

"When the Weather was poor, and this it was for long, we were put to considerable Trouble. Thus we had to stay down in the Lobster-pot if we did not wish forever to be soaking wet from walking on Deck, although it could not always be prevented, since now and then we had to get up, breathing a little fresh Air and stretching our Legs. However, the worst Nuisance, I believe, was the Stench from the Ship, which was made quite unbearable by the lurching and pitching of the Vessel. We felt worse, of course, in our Lobster-pot, as this was in closest Contact with the Hold. There was Sludge everywhere, making everything look as if it was painted or smeared with Stove Polish–even our Hands and Faces were black."

The World's First Arctic Magazine

Around the midle of the previous century the catches in Greenland deteriorated rapidly. At that time, Denmark was busily engaged in a war with her arch enemy to the south and, therefore, economically strained. Consequently, the Greenlanders suffered greatly. For long periods they simply did not have enough to eat, and gradually the population sank into permanent apathy and left more and more to the Danes.

Fortunately, there was a man in Godthaab who clearly saw the dangers threatening the primitive civilization in Greenland. This man was *H. J. Rink,* inspector for Southern Greenland and a well-known geologist. In an attempt to arouse the Greenlanders' interest in their own dying culture, he decided to publish a magazine in the Greenland language.

A printing house was established in Godthaab and on January 1st, 1861 "Atuagagdliutit" (meaning something offered for reading) was published for the purpose of "procuring for the Greenlanders some general Entertainment or Instruction". The first article told about the ships which had arrived at Godthaab harbour in 1860, but otherwise the magazine consisted mostly of stories from other parts of the world. Primarily, the magazine was meant to be a source of diversion in order to accustom the Greenlanders to reading.

"Atuagagdliutit" became the first magazine of the arctic world. It passed from hand to hand, and its beautiful coloured reproductions were hung on the walls in the earthen houses.

Little by little the magazine began to concern itself with the problems in Greenland. At the same time it became very patriotic, thanks especially to its first editor, Rasmus Berthelsen, who was also head catechist and teacher at the Seminary. He wrote hymns too, among them "Guterput" which became the national hymn of Greenland.

Through "Atuagagdliutit" the Greenlanders were informed about the strange and wonderful world which surrounded them. The used printing press, purchased for 250 rix-dollars, produced the colourful stories of Indians hunting on the American prairie, of cannibals and of Denmark where people had trees

Formidable Indian legends from the strange land of America were part of the amusing material in "Atuagagdliutit".
The accompanying lithographies were done by Lars Møller

The magazine's first masthead, showing Godthaab church

abundant with fruit. The magazine also brought the story of Robinson Crusoe.

But most important were the Greenlanders' own legends. The magazine brought tales from everyday life–unusual hunting experiences, dangerous trips in kayak and fights with bears. One of these is reproduced here:

Once we were holding a Prayer Meeting at Mathaeus' House, after which Benjamin's Son, who was the first to leave the House after the Sermon, immediately came rushing back crying out loud: That a big Bear was standing outside the House eating from the Blubber."

Mathaeus was delighted and grabbed a knife. The women tried in vain to hold him back. "The Women then undid their Hair Tops and spread out their Hair so that the Bear should think they were Men and for this Reason show more Fear and keep away from them."

"A Woman staggered back and forth across the Floor, all the while weaving a Couple of Straws together: This, they said, should serve to weaken the Bear's Strength (maybe make it dizzy)."

Matthaeus succeeded in getting down to his kayak where he kept his rifle.

"The Bear and Mathaeus stared fixedly into each others Faces, each from his Side of the Kayak. Mathaeus made Faces at the Bear, and it roared with its Jaws wide open, but now Mathaeus put his Foot hard against the Kayak and fired. Thereafter he buried his Seal Lance in it. Then he cried in a loud Voice up to the House that by all means they should come down and get their "ningek" (flensing pieces). The summoned Women, in their Eagerness to get past each other, were almost stuck in the narrow Corridor of the House, of which they broke several Pieces. When they reached the Bear, they all buried their Hands in the Wound and drank the Blood thereof, and all the while each

Woman called out the Part of the Animal which she wanted for a Flensing Piece."

"Before they started to flense, they drummed on the Bear Skin, while crying out loud: You are fat, fat, nice and fat," which is done in Politeness, since Bears as a Rule used to be fat, but when we started to open this one, it was found to be unusually skinny."

When they started to eat, the narrator cut the nose of the Bear's Head. The others were shocked.

"They assured me in all Seriousness that now I would never again catch a Bear, to which I answered them, that this in all Probability would come true, because I was so near-sighted that the Bear would come up and lick me, before I would notice it."

The story of Robinson Crusoe ran over three years and was accompanied by several illustrations. In Greenland he was called Krusoe, because they do not have the letter "C"

71

Arqaluk as Editor

In 1857 Rink employed a 15-year old Greenland boy by the name of Lars Møller to help in the newly established publishing house. The boy, who was better known by the name of Arqaluk, which means the older sister's younger brother, had lived a carefree hunting life and he was an unusually good kayak paddler and reindeer hunter.

However, Rink had discovered that Arqaluk was an exceptionally intelligent boy, and therefore he persuaded him into starting at the printing house as an apprentice.

Some years later Arqaluk was sent to Denmark for a short period of time to get some education and here he learned lithography. Inspector Rink, who was also a well-known scientist, was often invited to parties in the fashionable circles of Copenhagen and he always took Arqaluk along. The culmination was reached when Rink and Arqaluk, on the boy's birthday it so happened, were invited to Fredensborg to visit king Frederic VII, who wanted to see the Greenlander.

Upon seing Arqaluk, the king said: "I believe this is the first time I have seen a Greenlander." To which Arqaluk glibly remarked: "Come to think of it, this is the first time I have seen a king."

In 1874 Arqaluk took over the editorial post at "Atuagagdliutit", and for almost two generations he edited the magazine. But he did more than that.

Arqaluk, alias Lars Møller, drawn by Andreas Kornerup

He also made the illustrations, bound the magazine and mailed it to the most distant settlements.

Together with the most eminent artist Greenland has ever fostered–the primitive hunter Aron from Kangeq–he created a magazine which caused a stir everywhere in the civilized world. In it was published the first original art and literature from the Eskimo world.

During his summer trips Arqaluk collected stories about the experiences of his countrymen, and these he published in the magazine. The Greenlanders called it the "fun magazine", even though nearly every story was about death and misfortune, told simply and straight forward, without sensationalism and dramatic effects.

Most of the contributions began like this, ". . . since it is so much fun to read Atuagagdliutit, I, too, wish to come forward with my contribution . . ."

On the opposite page we give an example of such a dramatic story written by a Greenlander.

When Hans Egede talked about the Garden of Eden, not very many understood him, because none of the Greenlanders had ever seen a garden–and what was the tree of knowledge? But Arqaluk showed his readers what a garden was in Denmark, the promised land: There they pick an abundance of fruits from the trees and the bushes

72

The Umiak Loss

By Ignatius

They were ten in the Umiak which Ignatius had just built, and actually they were just on a Trial Run into Grædefjorden (The Weeping Fjord). It was September the 26th, 1890. Apart from Ignatius the following persons were on board the Boat, his Mother, the Widow Eleonora, Elisabeth, Priscilla, Jonas, Martha, Pauline, the Widow Christina, Rachel, 6 years of age, and Samuel-Mathaeus. Everything went well until October 5th when New Ice started to form. They began rowing towards Home, but they ran into a Storm.

"Immediately I gave Order to heave to, but we were very quickly carried towards an Iceberg and at the same Time we were fouled by the breaking New Ice which the Storm carried towards us, and the Umiak immediately sprung a Leak and began to sink. I heard one of the Women Rowers cry out: "I wonder if God, Our Creator, will not look down upon us at all?" During the Whistling of the Storm, however, and the Crashing Noise of the Boat, I could not distinguish who it was that spoke. Now I, Ignatius, hurriedly set out my Kayak, but right away it was pressed under the many Ice Floes, and only by exerting all my Strength I succeeded in pulling it back, but Jonas and I had barely seated ourselves each in his own Kayak, before we saw the Umiak sink before our very Eyes.

At the same time I felt something touch me on my Shoulder, and when I turn around, I saw that it was Martha, but She was caught by a Wave and disappeared immediately, and now we two Kayak Men also began to sink, cut by the Ice, and as we slowly sank into the Ocean, I heard Jonas pray: 'Jesus, come and stay with me. Your Wounds shall be my Comfort - I love You'.

Now they have all gone to the Bottom, I thought, as I came up to the Surface again, after I had worked myself out of the Kayak under the Water, but it was not so, because soon after I spotted Martha and then Elisabeth, my own Wife, and our old Servant, Priscilla, but all the others were gone together with Jonas, because he, in contrast to me, was caught in his Kayak.

Then Elisabeth says across to me: 'Yes, now God will dissolve our Marriage in Death,' and immediately she was carried away. Now Priscilla and I were alone among the Waves. I lifted my hands towards the Heaven and cried: 'God be merciful to me, Your Sinner,' I had been able to lift myself up by the Help of a Bundle of Skins which came floating to meet me, and which I soon recognized to have been my own Mother's. The Steering Oar came also floating to me, I kept myself above Water to the Chest. Once again Priscilla appeared on Top of a Wave, and I heard her say, 'This is terrible. Now I am sure it is my Turn.'

'Yes, you speak the Truth, when you say it is terrible,' I answered her, 'But whomever of us - whether it is going to be You or me - is either going to be punished or pardoned, No One knows.' And then I repeated my Prayer as before. She, the old Woman whom I least of all had thought should live, lived the longest. She did not die until Midnight, and her Death was not Drowning, because she had breathed her last just before she went down. Soon another Bundle of Travelling Clothes came rushing towards me, and I recognized it as Martha's. Finally I got it open and took out her little Featherbed, in which I tore a Couple of Holes, so that I could pull it over me.

Later on I came up on Top of an Ice Floe and drifted along in the Storm with both Legs sticking into the Water to the Middle of my Thighs. I prayed constantly, even though I remembered that God was Allmighty and in any Case would only act according to his own Will.

At last I reached Land and after three Days and Nights I got back the Use of my frozen Limbs. The only Food I had was a Razorbill, which I ate raw. Finally a Brother of Jonas and Martha found me. Both the Brother and later the Parents, who lost two of their Children in the Shipwreck, received me gently and kindly, I who was to blame for their having lost their two dear Children. For this happy Issue, I had to praise God."

An Eyewitness Account Anno 1863

The gay stories in ATUAGAGDLIUTIT and the colourful illustrations could not, however, disguise the fact that the Greenlanders had become an impoverished people. In 1865, *E. Bluhme,* a lieutenant in the Navy, who had lived in Greenland in 1863-64, fired a torpedo against the Danish government. He revealed the true conditions in detail, and cursed both the trading company and the mission.

He writes about a visit to a hut: "Bent over, steadying ourselves with our Hands, we crawl in, push the low, poorly fitting Door aside, but as we came from the Daylight, we could at first see nothing, since the Lamps have been put out for Months already for the Lack of Blubber. I could not stand up inside, the Water was dripping from the Roof. The Mud reached over my Foot. The Hut was approximately twelve Feet wide, twice as long and filled with People of all Ages, particularly Women, since three Widows lived there, two of them being the Mothers of two newly drowned young People. Do you all sleep here, I asked. Yes, was the Answer; they were some and twenty in all. The one Widow sat quietly crying, it

was only a short Time since she had lost her oldest Son. She stopped her Tears for a moment to point at her youngest Son, a boy of seven years, and said: He wants so much to eat.

The other Widow's grief was older, but equally deep, you could tell that from the hopeless Look in her Eyes. She said Nothing, sat still with her Hand under her Chin and stared straight ahead. And to complete this sad Picture, the third Widow sat behind her on her Knees on the bare stone bed. She rocked restlessly back and forth–she was blind. No One worked, they owned Nothing, not even a few Skins and some Thread made of Sinews, so that they could sew a Pair of Kamiks.

A Piece of old Sole Skin, bound around the naked Foot with a Piece of Twine was All they had for walking in the Snow at 15° below Freezing. Bedclothes they had not: As they sat during the Day in their Rags so they went to sleep at Night and their Food consisted of a Bit of Flour–which they had begged–stirred into some Water, a little Seaweed and Fish, maybe a Bird–and most often Everything had to be eaten raw."

Bluhme proves how poverty has spread everywhere on the coast. He blames the trading company for having exhausted the population so that they hardly have a shirt on their back. The gay nomadic people have become sendentary because of trade and the missionaries. They can no longer make kayaks and umiaks, because they do not catch anything and have no skins.

One of the main reasons for this misery can be found in the trading company regulations, Bluhme says. Part of the regulations read like this,

§ 2: Whosoever, without due Cause, neglects to attend Morning and Even-

This is how a German artist saw the Greenlanders' misery a hundred years ago

The shabby, but enthusiastic Greenlanders are gathering around some music boxes given to them by a German expedition

Not all Greenlanders lived in poverty. An inside look from a home in Jakobshavn anno 1847. Drawing by C. Rudolph

ing Prayers, or the Sunday Sermon, pays for the first Time 8 Skilling, the second Time double, etc. However, if he is found to have been drunk, has committed something improper, or during Prayers has disturbed Someone in his Devotions by Laughter, Noise, Cursing etc. he will be punished on his Purse or his Body.

§ 3: Since the Greenlanders' and the Greenland Women's all too frequent and free relations with the wintering Sailors, Colonists and other Europeans in the Country have given Rise to Laziness, Neglect of Duties, Lavishness, Debauchery and much Disorderliness, the following must be observed for that purpose:

a) The Europeans must not take just any Greenland Woman they please to serve them, sew their clothes and do their housework.

b) Young Greenland Woman are forbidden to go on Boat Cruises.

c) The Inhabitants must not, under severe Penalty, be made drunk from Beer and other European Drinks. Neither must they be spoiled with Coffee, Tea and other European Things, since such will harm their Health, ruin their Way of Living and give Them a Taste for idling in the European Houses. Aquavit must never be served to Women; the fine being 10 rix-dollars.

About the observance of the regulations Bluhme adds: "Each Day Aquavit is served all over Greenland. In the Godthaab District this year (1863), Goods have been bought in the Country for 1000 rix-dollars and in the same period Coffee has been sold for almost 1200 rix-dollars."

The coffee drinking, he finds, is the worst. The population has been exploited by offering them coffee. As an example, he mentions a visit to an earth hut where the rain was pouring down from the ceiling, and where the only thing protecting the half-naked, ragged and hungry dwellers, was one single piece of skin. The only thing they owned. They tried to sell him the skin in return for a little coffee.

Bluhme feels that the trading company had started out with the best intentions: Distribution of Danish foods was prohibited, except in case of famine or illness, but this decision was undermined from within. In 1804 rewards were given to the best hunters in the form of coffee and sugar. On the king's birthday European provisions were distributed in the settlements.

When whale flensing took place, aquavit was served to everyone. The youngest, who did not like it, saved it in their mouth and later they gave it to the others, by the simple mouth-to-mouth method.

The Greenland people were beginning to disintegrate.

When Nature is Generous

Lieutenant Bluhme painted Greenland very black. On the other hand, nature and life itself could also be painted in gay pastels, gentle and generous as shown in these colour pictures from the 1850's by H. J. Rink and in the drawings from the more rugged Northern Greenland.

The long, cold winter, hunger and death is forgotten when the warm fjords abound with salmon, berries and flowers and, on the breaking ice in the North, with seal and walrus. Forgotten, too, is the cliff from which the old ones threw themselves, when they were left to die from starvation anyway. This world of summer abundance is probably–rather than the helpfulness of the Danes–the explanation why the Greenlanders survived, in the North as well as in the South, even though the terms of their survival are far from identical. There is as much difference between life in Northern and Southern Greenland as there is between living on Baffin Island and in Mexico and the distance is just about the same.

This is Southern Greenland when life is best. Excursion to Qornoq in Godthaab Fjord 1863

The young must learn the life of a hunter   *Walrus hunting in Northern Greenland one hundred years ago*

*The lake at Tasermiut in Southern Greenland. The Greenlanders have hauled an umiak
all the way up to the lake to catch salmon and shoot reindeer*

Summer life near Kajutak in Godthaab Fjord. They are collecting wood and berries 77

The Spirits Protect Them

There are hundreds of Greenland myths and legends describing strange occurrences. A few myths are directly relating to the clash with the Norsemen, but many others, the majority, are about the struggle against the invincibility of nature.

Through a period of seven years, inspector Rink collected myths and legends and in the course of three winters he translated them with the help of Rasmus Berthelsen, the assistant teacher at the Seminary in Godthaab. It amounted to a total of 350 stories, but as he found numerous repetitions in the stories, the number was finally reduced to 170. They were first printed in the colony printing house in Godthaab between 1859 and 1863 under the title "Kaladtlit Okalluktualliait", and later published by H. J. Rink in "Eskimo tales and myths".

The myths are influenced by the world surrounding the Greenlanders–the ocean, the ice, the animals. And, naturally, the supernatural powers, the eerie.

The supernatural powers are often friendly. They help the Greenlander, who has always lived on the brink of existence, struggling for the daily necessities, and against the intruding strangers. This applies all the way from the mysterious legends about the Inland People to the more realistic tales about the whalers.

Even the weakest soul in the Greenland community has a spirit for an ally. This goes in particular for the widows and the fatherless children. The old and weak men know how to make tupilakker, which can chase and kill their enemies, and the women have their ways to protect and avenge the wronged.

The hunters are protected by spirits living among the rocks along the beach, and if a kayak man dies, he will awaken again at the bottom of the sea where he is received in his grandparents' arms.

Aron from Kangeq and Jens Kreutzmann have made the illustrations here.

Some of the Greenland stories are rather racy: "The wise man puts back a voman's soul through the anus. It had been stolen from her by a bad spirit."

The old Greenland game with a stuffed seal is part of many legends

The bristle worm (snake?) is mentioned in many Greenland legends. Here a woman is getting offspring with the help of the bristle worm

Several legends tell of blood feuds—here out at sea

"When Paulina discovered that his wife had a bachelor for her lover, he ordered his dog to pull them both apart. Now all the housemates started to run not realizing that P had no intention of letting the innocent come to any harm, and this the clever dog knew too, all by itself."

The great merman lives in the ocean. Here Qivakiarssuk is talking to him

An "aussik" chasing a sled. The aussik is a supernatural animal, a snake or a worm

Jens K.

Avarunguak, it is told, was rather surprised when he brought home his first walrus, and the woman in the house where he had been living took it with one hand and dragged it home. Not until later did Avarunguak discover that he had wintered with a bear family who had taken human form

The story of Nakasung who did not want to hide in the tent when the big mosquitoes came. Later, the others found Nakasung's skeleton

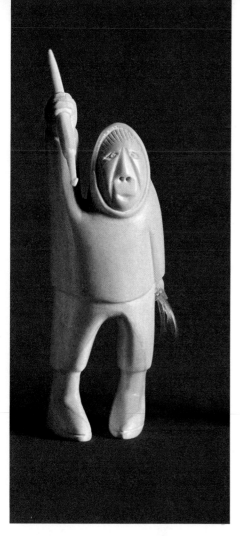

From the story of Kunuk the strong. The Norse chieftain (in white) is lashing him with a walrus whip, but Kunuk is none the worse for the whipping.
On a later occasion the invincible Kunuk wrestles with series of opponents, defeating them all

The Records of a Greenland Pastor

The church always had a very strong hold on the Greenland population. One may speculate as to why this is so, but possibly the Danish pastor Carl Emil Janssen, in his book "The Records of a Greenland Pastor 1844-49", comes very close to the truth: "The Church is the only spiritual Source from which they can draw some Satisfaction, and therefore, it would seem to me a great Sin against them if we, in that Respect, showed Indifference or Neglect.

Among themselves the Greenlanders do not seem to know Hate or Envy, Enmity, Persecution or Strife, and you never hear about Fights, Violence, Robberies or Murder; they have no Locks on their Doors, they have no closed Closets or Chests. And though, here I might be showing a mistaken Enthusiasm; this is daily in my Thoughts. Maybe their Ignorance is causing them to stay in a Sort of natural State of Simple-mindedness which looks like Virtue. The harsh Climate, their few Necessities, and the hard Way in which they must obtain these, possibly keep them in this peaceful State of Equality. One seldom knows more than the other, one seldom owns more than the other, and therefore they find no Occasion to elevate themselves. They must help others in order to get Help themselves."

Empty church pews are an unknown sight in Greenland. The only time might be when the cry "whales!" run through the colony. Then the pastor is left alone in his church, but if he has lived in Greenland long enough, he will rush down from his pulpit, too, and take part in the catch. Be as it may, God will have to wait a little.

C. E. Janssen writes about a Christmas sermon in the old Greenland: "All the Children of the Settlement, dressed in brand new Clothes, crowded around the Church and the Houses of the Danes. The Pastor was standing in his Door distributing a Pieces of Hardtack to each of the dressed-up Children.

When Rumours of the Distribution spread through the Houses, the Mothers came running with the little Ones on their Backs.

At six o'clock the Church was lit with 20 Lamps, and all the Greenlanders were present in their very best Clothes: all the Women in their high, red Boots and many-coloured Fancy Work down their Breeches; Silk Ribbons around their high Topknots, looking more like a Regiment of Guardsmen than a flock of females ... A blue Ribbon around the Topknot signifies that the Woman is married; the Maidens carry a red Ribbon and unmarried Women with Children a green Ribbon."

Festive costumes from Greenland. Woodcut by Rasmus Berthelsen. From the book "Kaladtlit assilialiait" (Greenland Woodcuts) published in Godthaab 1858

The Church and the doctor's house in Jakobshavn. Watercolour by C. Rudolph. The doctor's house probably has the most beautiful view in the world, overlooking the fjord where new icebergs are born every few minutes

The services are over.
Lithography by Lars Møller, published in "Atuagagdliutit"

Names Written in the Perpetual Snows

From the earliest times Greenland has called forth the spirit of inquiry in all the peoples of the world. Eric the Red and his landnamsmen were the very first explorers. After them followed the whalers. Systematic exploration did not begin, however, until the 16th century when the polar explorers sought a short cut to India and China.

Through centuries the ambition of thousands was to find the Northwest Passage or one to the Northeast, and countless human tragedies took place here at the top of the earth. Those who turn the pages of the long history of the Greenland expeditions will wonder at the amount of human suffering, self-sacrifice and courage it has taken to fill the many white spots on the Greenland map.

The people involved in this century-long arctic drama were far from being heroes. Some were honest and courageous, some were fools. Countless of them found their grave under the perpetual snow. But their memory will never die - their names are forever written in the never melting snow.

The First Expeditions Begin

"Nowhere else has knowledge been paid for with greater amounts of hardship, suffering and distress, but the human spirit will not rest until every spot in these regions have been laid under human foot and every mystery solved."

Fridtjof Nansen

Even though Greenland was Danish, it was also international. Outside the peaceful, somewhat sleepy colonies, settlements and trading stations, where time went on as usual, there was a dramatic world, the world of the expeditions. As a rule they had no great contact with the colonies, but they are part of the history of Greenland and they form a very interesting chapter. English, American, French, German, Austrian-Hungarian, Norwegian and Swedish expeditions risked their lives to fill the white spots on the map of Greenland. There are still untouched white spots. Not only on the Ice Cap but also thoughout the vast regions of Eastern Greenland. They can be photographed from airplanes and satellites or men can be put ashore from helicopters, and you can send atomic submarines up through the ice exactly at the spot where the North Pole is, but not even a thousand years of explorations have been able to wrest all the mysteries from Greenland.

The very first arctic explorer in history was Sir *Hugh Willoughby* who pushed his way through the ice masses north of Norway in 1553. He committed the first arctic errors. In his instructions to the sailors he wrote that they should beware of the swimming, naked, man-like monsters who can eat up the ships. Mistake followed upon mistake, but also victory upon victory.

During the following centuries, arctic exploration developed into an arctic drama of proportions. Countless found their deep-frozen grave on the Ice Cap. Their names can still be read on the map. It is no matter for surprise that many of them were English, as they were

looking for the Northwest Passage long before anyone else. *Martin Frobisher* was the first in 1576, *John Davis* the second in 1585.

In 1607 *Henry Hudson,* sent out by the Moskow Company in London, tried, as the first, to push through to the North Pole. 575 nautical miles from the top of the earth he had to give up, and 166 years were to pass before others reached this high up north. This intrepid explorer, who discovered Spitsbergen and Jan Mayen, suffered a sad fate in the enormous bay which bears his name, Hudson Bay. Led on by the first officer the crew mutinied. Hudson, his son and five members of the crew were put out in a lifeboat and perished. Later four of the instigators of the mutiny were killed by the Eskimos, but the survivors, who returned to England, escaped the gallows only because they could show the way to these newly discovered arctic regions. During a later expedition they sailed north along the westcoast of Greenland, and the first officer on the DISCOVERY, *William Baffin,* lent his name to Bafin Bay. They found a sound north of Thule which they called Smith Sound after Sir *Thomas Smith* who had been one of the financers of the expedition. Centuries later this sound became the access to the North Pole. They also found two more sounds which were named after other benefactors, Jones Sound and Lancaster Sound which 236 years later were to be the chief aim of the exploration of the Northwest Passage. Here the greatest tragedies that arctic exploration has known took place.

Among those who found death instead of China, were 62 members of the Danish expedition 1619-20, com-

*In 1827 Edward Parry tried to reach the
North Pole from Spitsbergen but he had
to turn back 560 miles from the goal*

*Parry's expedition 1819-20 met enormous
icebergs in Baffin Bay*

*"The sailors should beware of the
swimming, naked man-like monsters that
could eat up the ships . . ."*

*A British account of Jens Munk's travels shows this picture of whaling
"under Spitsbergen"; actually they meant Greenland*

87

A strange world revealed itself to the European explorers looking for the Northwest Passage. The picture shows a village with snow huts, Eskimos with snow glasses made out of wood. These very instructive illustrations were shown in Parry's travel accounts, which were published in London in 1824

manded by *Jens Munk*. With two ships and 64 men he searched the Hudson Bay for the Northwest Passage. Only Munk and two other survived, and after terrible sufferings they returned to Denmark, where an unsympathetic king gave Munk a slap on his chest with his stick, when he wanted to make another voyage. The infuriated explorer returned home, went to bed and refused to take any nourishment. Ten days later he died from starvation and bitterness.

For a couple of centuries the whalers had the polar regions almost to themselves; then began a new search for the Northwest Passage because of the growing jealousy among the colonial powers over the expansion of Russia.

After the Dane *Vitus Bering* had shown the way through the strait between Asia and America, the Russians pushed down into Alaska and America —all the way to San Francisco. And now the English were afraid that the Rus-

Wintering in the icy wastes, 1819. The ships are Parry's HECLA *and* GRIPER

89

sians would also appropriate the arctic regions of Canada. Furthermore, everyone had a surplus of men and officers after the Napoleonic Wars. In 1818, *John Ross* was sent up through the Davis Strait, where he could only verify Baffin's discoveries 202 years earlier. He pushed into Lancaster Sound, but suddenly turned back, because he thought he had seen mountains which would block his way. This must have been an optical illusion. Ross quarrelled with his officers who wanted to continue, and when he returned home a sharp debate arose on the question of these mountains. In 1819 the admiralty decided to send out another expedition under the command of *Edward Parry,* who

had been next in command under Ross. He quickly proved that Ross had been mistaken and pushed his way into arctic Canada. Years later, in 1827, he tried to reach the North Pole from Spitsbergen by pulling two small boats across the ice. He reached a point less than 560 miles from the North Pole. In 1829 John Ross, who sought compensation for his defeat, started on a new expedition with the sailing ship VICTORY. This was no success either. The most important result of the four year long voyage, during which Victory had to be left in the ice, was the discovery of the magnetic north pole. This discovery was made by John Ross' nephew *James Clark Ross.* He was offered the command of a

new expedition but refused because he had promised his wife to stay at home. The task was assigned to Sir *John Franklin* who accepted even though he was nearly 60 years old.

It was one of the biggest mistakes in arctic exploration of that day to send out elderly people into the wilderness. Another was that apparently the British fleet had not yet learned to equip their ships according to the demands of the situation. Great importance was attached to regulations, to fifes and drums and traditions instead of paying attention to absolute necessities.

The British fleet was not prepared for walking. That is why the expedition became a death march.

The Canadian Eskimos looked somewhat different from the Greenland Eskimos. The women were tattooed and their clothes were more draped. A drawing from Edward Parry's description 1824

90

A ship stuck in the ice with all hands out. The picture gives an impression of the hardships of sailing through the ice

They Pulled Their Noses
as a Sign of Peace

John Ross was probably the first European who had direct contact with the arctic Eskimos, the Thule people, when –in 1818–he tried to find the Northwest Passage with the same negative result as fifty others before him. With him on the expedition was Hans Zakaeus, a young Greenlander whom John Ross had met in Leith. Zakaeus grew up at a mission station in Disko Bay, but later on he ran away to sea and came with a ship to Scotland. Here he learned to paint–a couple of his pictures are presented on this and the following pages. John Ross did not find the Northwest Passage, but he met the original Thule Eskimos. This meeting took place on the ice near Prince Regent Inlet and it developed into quite a pantomime.

John Ross writes that at first he thought they were some shipwrecked sailors standing on the ice, but then it dawned on him that they were natives and he called for Zakaeus. He was given a white flag and some gifts, but the Eskimos kept at a distance of approx. 300 yards. The British ran up a big flag, showing the sun and the moon over an outstretched hand, holding a heather plant; to the mast was tied a bag with gifts while sign with a hand pointed towards the ship.

Zakaeus gesticulated, he flourished his hat and waved, and finally some of the natives dared to come nearer. The most courageous of the Eskimos finally walked up to Zakaeus, pulled out a knife and said: "Get out. I can kill you!" Zakaeus threw a British knife to him. He picked it up, examined it, called something to the others and began to pull his nose. Immediately Zakaeus did the same and in the end everyone was pulling his nose. Pulling your nose was considered a sign of friendship among the Eskimos.

Captain Ross came forward with gifts, the Eskimos did likewise, and they let themselves be invited on board the ships where the British found out that Eskimoes hate plum pudding and aquavit. The next day the expedition sailed on and the arctic Eskimos drove off on their sleds.

Eleven years later, John Ross was again in Greenland in his endless search for the Northwest Passage. Once more he met with the arctic Eskimos and befriended them, especially as he let his carpenter cut a wooden leg for one of the Eskimos who had lost his.

The memory of John Ross' visit still lived on in the Thule Eskimos' legends almost one hundred years later, when the Danish arctic explorer Knud Rasmussen came to the settlement. He writes that a woman by the name of

The meeting with the arctic Eskimos in Prince Regent Inlet in 1818. The picture is painted by Hans Zakaeus

94   *The British winter camp on the ice. There was no shortage of flags and festoons in the long arctic nights*

Nauja had prophesied that a big boat with high stanchions would come into sight from the ocean. An one summer day an »island of wood« came alongside the ice. It moved across the sea with wings and had many houses and rooms deep in its belly with many noisy people. Little boats were hanging along the edge, and when these were filled with people and lowered into the water it was as if the monster brought forth its young.

The visit caused fear and horror. The Eskimos did not believe that the white men were real people, but thought they were spirits of the air that had flown down to the land of the Greenlanders.

*During its second expedition to Greenland,
VICTORY ran into a gale which cut off the
top of the foremast. The ship was
pressed down by the ice. It took four years
of hardship before the 22 sailors were
rescued and sailed back home*

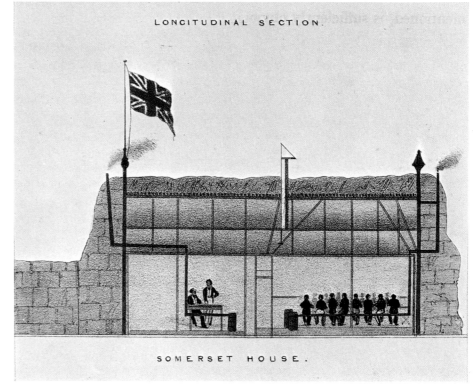

Cross section of Somerset House, the main building of the winter camp on the ice

The Mysterious Disappearance of 129 Men

Very possibly a British provision swindler was the cause of the biggest and most ghastly arctic tragedy during the 19th century–which took the lives of 129 men.

On May the 10th, 1845 two warships, EREBUS and TERROR, left England with the same operational orders as countless others before them: Find the Northwest Passage.

In command was Sir John Franklin, renowned explorer and one of the heroes of the Battle of Trafalgar, 1805.

One would have thought that he had enough of arctic voyages. During an expedition twenty years earlier in the Hudson Bay area Franklin had seen his men eat another sailor, and he had to use all his authority to prevent several more members of the expedition from being disposed of. This time, in the early spring of 1845, he felt sure that this would never happen again. He carried provisions for at least 3½ years. And on July 26th when meeting another British ship, PRINCE OF WALES, which was on its way home, he stated that he figured on having provisions enough for five years or more. That was how many birds his men had shot during the voyage. While the ships were moored to an iceberg, seven of the officers paid a visit to Sir John, at which time he reported all well on board.

From this day on nothing was heard from the expedition. The fate of the two ships went down in history as a terrible tragedy.

When two years had passed with no word from the Franklin expedition, the British government, hard pressed by the public feelings, took the initiative to a search. 20,000 pound Sterling was offered as a reward to whoever could rescue Franklin, and Lady Franklin offered a reward of 3000 pounds. During the next ten years a total of forty British, French and American relief expeditions were sent out.

The first traces of Franklin were found in 1850. At that time 11 ships were gathered at the approach to the search area around the Wellington Channel. Here remains were found which suggested that the expedition had used the spot for a wintering base. They also found three crosses with the names of three members of the expedition, but no light was thrown on the fate of the rest.

During the following years numerous expeditions were sent out, and some of these got into such serious trouble that others had to be sent out to rescue them. Finally, in 1853 Commander *Robert McClure,* R. N., and H. M. S. ENTERPRISE found the Northwest Passage–but not Franklin.

One of the unlucky expeditions was commanded by Sir Edward Belcher. He lost four ships in the pack ice. When he returned to England he was court-martialled–but acquitted.

The arctic explorer Dr. John Rae was more lucky. In 1854 he was sent out by the Hudson Bay Company and late in the summer he was able to send the British Admiralty the sensational message that he had found definite traces of the Franklin expedition. On King William Island he had talked with an Eskimo who four years earlier had seen nearly 40 white men with a boat and some sleds. Later in the summer the Eskimos had found more than 30 dead bodies and some graves, and on an island near the mouth of the Back or Fish River they had found the bodies of five more members of the expedition. They had died from starvation. The Eskimos could see that they had tried to eat each other.

The information about cannibalism among the British naval officers created quite a stir–and a good deal of indignation–in London. People found it utterly

*Thus they »buried«
their dead
in the Arctic Ocean*

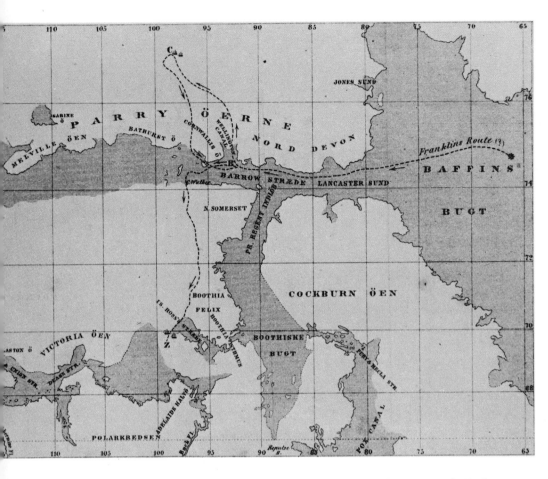

△ *This is how uncomplicated the map looked when the search was started. Nothing more was known at that time, but ten years later the map looked quite different* ▽

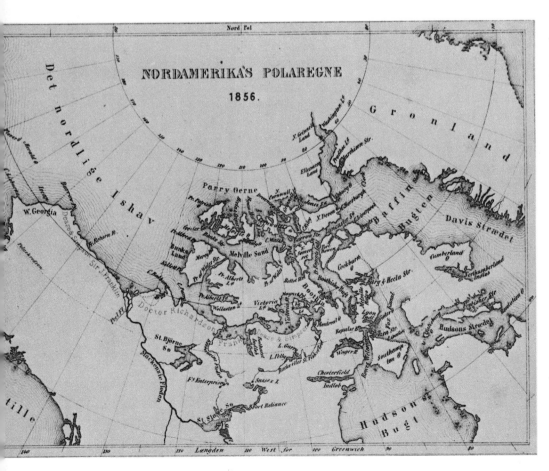

Sir John Franklin, Governor of New Holland, was selected, despite his high age (59 yrs.), to command the great search for the Northwest Passage

Two years after Franklin's disappearance the British government appointed a committee which should work on solving this mystery. This committee consisted of celebrities from previous arctic expeditions, among them were Edward Parry (2nd from the left) and James Clark Ross (fourth from the left). The portrait on the wall at right shows Sir John Barrow

incomprehensible that British gentlemen could even *think* of eating each other.

From the Eskimos Dr. Rae bought a lot of things which had belonged to the Franklin expedition, for instance silver with Franklin's and several of his officers' monograms. Because of this discovery Dr. Rae received half of the reward which had been offered for information about Franklin. At the same time, Commander McClube and his crew received 10,000 pound Sterling, or half of the amount offered for the discovery of the Northwest Passage.

It was still very uncertain, however, if all the members of the Franklin expedition had perished. A few new expeditions sought in vain to solve the mystery, and after 12 years of costly, dangerous searches with 40 ships and more than a thousand men at stake, the British prime minister, Lord Palmerston, finally gave up. No more searches.

Lady Franklin, on the other hand, refused to give up hope, and in the summer of 1875 she equipped the small

screw steamer FOX with the famous captain McClintock in command and a Dane, Carl Petersen, as pilot and interpreter. This was the fourth time that Lady Franklin sent out an expedition at her own expense.

The 44-year old Carl Petersen had been living in Upernavik for a number of years, where he was a foreman while his wife worked as a midwife. He had been a member of several of the expeditions which had tried to solve the Franklin mystery.

99

The FOX had a total of 26 persons on-board and they managed to do what a thousand others had not been able to. The first trace of the Franklin expedition was an anchor button in the belt of an Eskimo. They bought it for a sewing needle. Later on they bought silver spoons, forks, and uniform buttons from other Eskimos. The price was still one sewing needle for each thing, no matter what the object was. The captain did not want to "spoil the market", as he said, by offering more for the various things.

The captain's worries were, in a sense, unnecessary because little by little the properties of the expedition were found on the many subsequent sledge voyages.

Dr. John Rae who received half of the reward

McClintock was the leader of the expedition which finally solved the mystery

Carl Petersen, wearing the Silver Cross of the Order of Dannebrog and the Royal Swedish Medal of Merit in gold. A dramatic life ending very peacefully, almost dully. For fourteen years Carl Petersen was a lighthouse keeper until he retired and moved to Copenhagen

FOX *in heavy pressure ice*

Also, three skeletons were found and –most important of all–an account hidden in a cairn. The letter said that Franklin died on June 11th 1847.

The Fox expedition demonstrated that Franklin had been offer for a provision swindle. A great many cans contained hair, skin, bone and other trash, but nothing eatable. On Beechey Island a whole pyramide of tin cans was found, which had not been emptied but just opened and left untouched. The supplier: Goulash manufacturer Goldner, London.

The search expedition spots the cairn which contained the sensational information about Sir Franklin's death

---

A shocking document

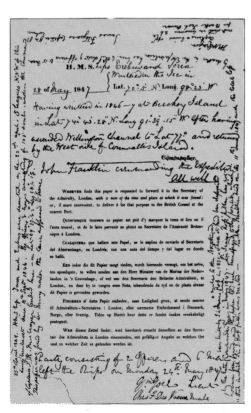

At left is seen a facsimile of the message which was found in a cairn by captain McClintock. In various languages (besides in English, the message is translated into French, Spanish, Dutch, Danish and German) the finder is requested to contact the Secretary of the Admirality in London or the British consul at the nearest port.

The handwritten text sounds as follows: "Having wintered in 1846-7 at Beechey Island in Lat. 74°43'.28" N. Long. 91.39'.15" W. After having ascended Wellington Channel to Lat. 77° and returned by the West side of Cornwallis Island.–Sir John Franklin commanding the Expedition. All well."

At the bottom is added: "Party consisting of 2 Officers and 6 Men left the ships on Monday 24th May 1847. Gm. Gore, Lieut. Chas F. Des Vaeux, Math."

On the left side the text reads: "25th April 1848. H. M. Ships TERROR and EREBUS were deserted on the 22nd April. 5 leagues NNW of this having been beset since 12th Sept. 1846. The Officers & Crew consisting of 105 Souls under the Command of Captain I. R. McCrozier landed here –in Lat. 69°37',42" Long 98°41. This paper was found by Lt. Irwing under the Cairn supposed to have been built by Sir James Ross in 1831 –4 miles to the Northward–where it had been deposited by the late Commander Gore in May 1847 . . . Sir Franklin died on the 11th June 1847 and the total loss of deaths on the Expedition has been to the date 9 officers & 15 men."

The document is signed by James Fitzjames, Captain H. M. Ship Erebus and I. R. McCrozier, who was the senior officer.

The very last notation written on this amazing document reads, ". . . and start on tomorrow 26th for Back Fish River."

One Man's Stubbornness

Of the many unsuccessful expeditions searching for Franklin, Dr. E. K. Kane's expedition with the brigantine ADVANCE was one of the most dramatic.

The ship sailed from New York on May 30th 1853 and on July 20th it took the Danish pilot, Carl Petersen, onboard in Upernavik. They continued northward past the present Thule all the way up to 78° 30' north.

Carl Petersen warned Dr. Kane that he was leading his ship into a death trap, but the stubborn leader of the expedition refused to turn around. He went into winter quarters further north than any other ship had ever done before. In March of the following year he gave orders that a sledge pulled by eight men should go north. The pilot protested, but Kane was unrelenting. Six days later the eight men returned, and one of them died shortly after. The cook had to have one foot amputated and two of the others lost some of their toes from frost bites.

In the early spring it was clear to everyone that ADVANCE would never come free of the ice. Heading a group of twelve men, Carl Petersen tried going south for help, but after having experienced the most terrible hardships, they had to turn back. They had to spend yet another winter on the ice without firewood and with very little in the way of provisions.

The relationship between the Danish pilot and Dr. Kane was by now as icy as the arctic cold. When Kane told Carl Petersen to warn an Eskimo that he would be shot if he did not obey a certain order, the pilot drew Kane's attention to the fact that since the ship was wrecked, his command might be considered revoked.

Contributing to the tension between the two was the ship's doctor Isaak Israel Hayes who turned out to be a scoundrel of the deepest dye. While Carl Petersen was away from the camp to get help, some Eskimos brought fresh provisions to the remaining Americans. Dr. Hayes gave them a dose of opium, and while they slept it off, he stole their skin clothes, giving them his own American rags instead. He also stole their dog sleds.

Dr. Hayes' view of the Cape York Eskimos is evident from his account of the expedition, published at a later time:

"The Eskimos are certainly a strange type of people and very interesting to study, even more so than my dogs, although they are not as useful. The dogs can be managed with firmness and a long whip, while the human animal cannot be managed by any such means. You could rightly so call them a negative people in everything, except in their untrustworthiness, which is absolutely positive."

In May of 1855 Dr. Kane finally gave up his hopes of getting his ship out of the ice. With the Danish pilot in command they went south and 81 days later the expedition reached Upernavik.

A man in a kayak was the first to spot them. Carl Petersen called to him: "Carl Zacharias, do you not know me? I am Carl Petersen!"

The kayakman looked horrified at him and answered: "No that is not true. His wife says that he is dead!" And then the kayakman paddled away for dear life from this ghost.

The rest of the story of the expedition is quickly told: "After having been lead to safety by Carl Petersen, the Americans were picked up by a relief expedition. Even though the relations between the pilot and Dr. Kane were rather strained during the rigours in the ice, Kane nevertheless gave Carl Petersen his due in the book he wrote about the expedition. He characterized him as a man of honor who risked his life time and again in order to save others.

Carl Petersen's wife, incidentally, went blind in her after years. The story goes that her tears did it. She had cried so much all the times she though that her husband would never return from his expeditions.

For 81 days and nights Carl Petersen led the expedition's two small boats south with 16 hungry American survivors. They had reached the point where they had decided to eat their last two dogs, when Petersen spotted a seal. Slowly, and foaming at the mouth, the starving, half-dead men approached the seal. Would it slip into water too early? The seal raised its head and Carl Petersen shot. Wild with hunger the men fell upon the dead seal. They ate it raw and greedily licked the blood off their fingers

The crew is trying to pull ADVANCE *free of the ice, but in vain*

Winter life onboard ADVANCE. *The elegant frock coats were not very well suited for temperatures of 50° below. Possibly that was the reason why Dr. Hayes stole the Eskimo's clothes*

Despite all the hardships the expedition also did scientific work. Here a picture of the expedition's somewhat primitive magnetic observatory

200 Days on a Drifting Ice Floe

On June 15th 1869 at exactly 3 p.m. Kaiser Wilhelm I of Prussia stood stiffly at the salute. Next to him stood the Grand Duke of Mecklenburg-Schwerin and the Iron Chancellor himself, Bismarck. The place was Bremerhaven and the occasion: the world's hitherto best equipped arctic expedition. The steamer GERMANIA and the schooner HANSA stood out of the harbor, carrying provisions for two years, in an attempt to add a new chapter to the history of arctic exploration. This turned out to be a dramatic chapter which began with a wreck and ended in success. Their aim was to explore the most northerly regions along the coast of Eastern Greenland and their ambition was to reach the North Pole and possibly go through the Northwest Passage.

The two ships sailed together, separated in storm and fog, were united in the ice masses of Eastern Greenland and then parted forever, because Captain Paul Hegemann on the HANSA misunderstood a signal from Captain Karl Koldeway on the GERMANIA. He signaled "come abreast" but this Hegemann understood as "go west". HANSA disappeared in the icy fog.

GERMANIA continued north and carried out a thorough exploration all the way up to Cape Bismarck. The crew wintered on the ice, making sled trips north. They explored and named this area, which almost 70 years later, during World War II, was to be chosen as the operational base for the German navy. Little did these German explorers know that they would enable Hitler's long arm to reach this far north. It was in this region the German and the Danish sled patrols fought so bitterly.

The crew from GERMANIA wintered on Sabine Island, exposed to the cold and numerous attacks from polar bears. One of the crew members was actually savaged by a bear. Approximately one year after their departure they arrived safely back home to Bremerhaven–to the war against France in 1870.

HANSA experienced a quite different voyage. The captain followed the misunderstood order and sailed due west, right into the ice trap of Eastern Greenland. On September 14th they were caught in Lat. 73° 25' N.

By September 27th HANSA's crew of 15 men thought that they might never leave the place. A few days earlier their ship had been pressed up on top of the ice. It was now lying 15 feet above the hard ice squeezed in by some huge blocks.

The crew hurriedly stripped the ship of everything. They even took the stove out. The last to leave the ship were the rats. They jumped out onto the ice in great numbers and died almost instantly from the cold.

On October 21st HANSA sank one and a half miles off the coast of Liverpool Land, and the crew wintered in an ice fort which they had built. Outside the fort lay three lifeboats–just in case.

And now the ice began drifting south. Their journey, which was rather bumpy, was to last 200 days. On November 3rd they were outside Scoresbysund. After having bungled several shots at bears, they finally caught one. Once they shot a female polar bear and tried to get a lasso around the cub, but they had bad luck and it ran away. Another time they also shot a female bear and this time they caught the cub with a lasso. They chained it to a ship's anchor and put the cable around its neck. Somehow, the cub succeeded in tearing the cable away from the anchor. The poor animal must have suffered a horrible death with the heavy cable weighing it down.

The crew from GERMANIA *exploring the wild mountains at Franz Joseph Fjord*

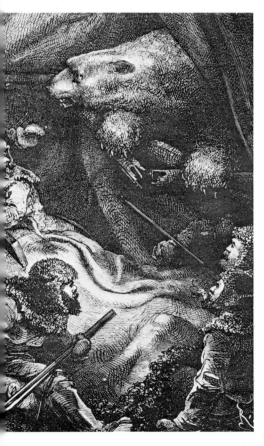

Wintering under the northern lights

Mock suns, an arctic phenomenon described by numerous expeditions from the past century

A polar bear broke into the tent

HANSA *stripped of everything*   *The bear cub tied to an anchor*

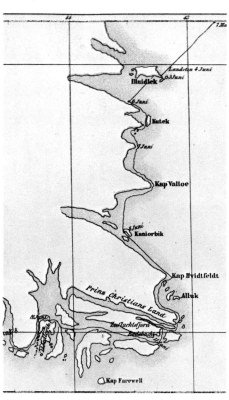

The route in the drift ice

The arrival at Frederiksdal. "We were welcomed in our mother tongue. Just think, a piece of our beloved Fatherland up here"

The Germans were still drifting south in winter storms and darkness. Somewhere north of Angmagssalik the ice floe started to break so that now their ice hut was no more than 200 feet from the edge. This happened off a bay which they named the Bay of Fear.

By now the ice floe was no more than 150 feet in diameter. One day at the beginning of March the ice split right through the house, but they still did not dare to take to the boats. A few days later, one of the participants in this fantastic voyage, Dr. Buchholtz, went insane.

On March 29th they recognized with excitement the coast line according to Graah's description of his expedition two years earlier.

On May 7th the rain was pouring down and the ice began to break. By simply majority vote it was decided to take to the boats. They had lived on the ice floe for 200 days and during the next four weeks they sailed among the ice in their small lifeboats.

On June 4th, for the first time since they left the ship, they felt solid ground under their feet, on the Island of Illuidlek. And, finally, on June 13th 1870 at four o'clock in the morning, they arrived with a fair wind and crowding whatever sails they had at the southernmost inhabited place in Greenland, namely Frederiksdal. To their great surprise, they were welcomed in their own language by the leader of the Moravian Brethren. Later they obtained passage from Frederikshaab to Copenhagen, arriving on December 1st.

Back in Germany they were received with flags flying. This, however, was not due to their conquest of the ice masses in Eastern Greenland, but to the German victory over the French.

Seven Kroner a Year to Teach the Children ABD

During the year-long search for the Franklin Expedition traffic was lively on the Greenland harbors. The arrival of foreign expedition ships was a welcome change in the monotonous everyday life in Greenland.

One of the most stubborn advocates of the theory that some of Franklin's men must have survived among the arctic Eskimos, was an American by the name of *Charles Francis Hall.*

In 1860 he arrived in Greenland with his ship GEORGE HENRY on his way to the Northwest Passage area. He put in at Holsteinsborg, among other things to find a new interpreter.

While in Holsteinsborg he held a dance on board and was in close contact with the local population. He gives a very precise description of conditions in Greenland at that time: "Only ten Danes lived in the town, and in all of Greenland there were only 250 among 9644 Eskimos, three fourths of whom have Danish (or American, British, French, Portuguese, Dutch or German) blood in them. The annual pay of the schoolmaster is 800 kroner (ca. 105 dollars), three other teachers each get 700 kroner. Four women who teach the children ABD (the letter C does not exist in the Greenland language) get seven kroner per year. 16 men employed by the government each get anywhere from 280 to 630 kroner annually plus their provisions. They have bread every two weeks.

Hall writes that his people expected to trade with the naïve natives, but there is at least one story of how they were cheated.

A Greenlander, whose name was Samson, turned up on board the ship and wanted to buy some tobacco from one of the crew members. He took out a bill from his pocket and as it said "sex Skilling" on it, the American thought it was equivalent to six Yankee Shillings (or almost two dollars). The sailor asked Samson how much tobacco he expected for the money. The Greenlander tried to explain that he wanted four slices, but the American misunderstood him and fetched four pounds (32 slices). The Greenlander was naturally rather surprised and slipped away in a hurry. All of a sudden he had become the richest man in Holsteinsborg.

After the visit to Holsteinsborg, the Hall expedition sailed north and stayed away for two years. The illustrations shown here are from Hall's book of the expedition which was successful, even though they suffered great hardships.

Hall's next expedition, on the other hand, turned into a drama which ended in murder.

The kamiks are being chewed so that they become soft and pliable. This was a woman's task

GEORGE HENRY *surrounded by Eskimos*

Dancing on board the American ship in Holsteinsborg

One of Hall's merits as an arctic explorer is that he found the place where Frobisher had camped 300 years earlier. The eskimos showed him the spot

After the happy days in Holsteinsborg the crew returned to the hard and lonely expeditionary life. The man with the stick is Hall

The Case of the Arctic Murder

"I've been poisoned. There was poison in the coffee." *Charles Francis Hall* lay in his cabin on board the POLARIS in the winter harbor approx. 81° north, in a small cove called "Gudskelov-havnen". (Thank God harbor). He suffered terribly from pains in his stomach. He had just returned from a sled trip toward the North Pole, and, weak from fatigue, he had drunk a refreshing cup of coffee in his cabin.

For two weeks he insisted that he had been poisoned with arsenic. Then, on November 8th, 1871, he died and was given a stately burial, wrapped in the American flag.

One hundred years later it was established that Francis Hall was right. He *was* murdered. In 1968, professor Chauncey Loomis and Franklin Paddock, a medico-legal expert, got permission to examine Hall's deep-frozen body, which had been buried under a stone cairn in a windswept, desolate area

Charles Francis Hall together with two Canadian Eskimos

The burial of Captain Charles Francis Hall. His ship POLARIS reached Lat 82°, higher north than any other ship before it. He pushed through the ice all the way up the arctic basin and named the channel between Greenland and Canada: Robeson Channel.
Then his luck changed. POLARIS, a 387-ton gunboat, old and better suited for river sailing, was stuck in the ice. Hall died from arsenic-poisoning, but his murderer or murderers gave him a stately burial, wrapped in the American flag

On August 7th 1968, professor C. C. Loomis opened Hall's grave and took this photograph of the deep-frozen body

north of Thule. Radioactive irradiation of Hall's fingernails revealed that without a doubt he had died from an overdose of arsenic.

This came one hundred years too late, however. The murderer or murderers–because in all probability they were two–have long since been carried to their graves, unpunished. The suspicion centers around the ship's master, the drunken Sidney Buddington and the expedition's German doctor, Dr. Emil Bessels who were constantly at loggerheads with Hall.

The POLARIS expedition was one of the most dramatic in the arctic history of the United States and Greenland. It had been equipped by the American government, and left with the President's personal blessing. Hall's aim (unofficially) was to sail to the North Pole. He worked his way through the Kane Basin and the Kennedy Channel easily enough. But where Greenland ended and the Arctic Ocean began the expedition met with an ice barrier. Aside from the British and American crew the ship had two Greenlanders on board, Hans Hendrik and Joe plus their families.

After Hall's death the expedition wintered, but on August 12th 1872 the ship came free of the ice. This did not last very long, though, soon it was stuck again and on October 12th a panic broke out. During a storm the crew had lost all faith in Captain Buddington. The officers started to throw the provisions overboard onto the ice, thinking that the ship was going to be wrecked. Ten Americans and nine Eskimos jumped down onto the ice, while Buddington and the rest of the crew stayed on board. POLARIS drifted away from the ice floe, once more it was stuck in the ice, and with the help of the Eskimos the remaining crew made a wintering hut. The following spring the ship drifted out into the open sea with no-

For one winter and one summer the POLARIS *was stuck in the ice. After that some of the officers did not want to play any longer. The captain stayed on board with the rest of the crew, while 19 men fled and started their fantastic voyage on an ice floe*

one on board.

At the beginning of the summer the crew sailed south toward Upernavik in small boats. Here they were lucky enough to be taken on board a Scottish whaler RAVENSCRAIG.

The 19 on the icefloe did not do so well, however, drifting south as they did. The white men were unable to manage by themselves and they submitted completely to the two Eskimo hunters who provided the necessary fresh supplies. They built a snow hut on the ice, and here they lived for more than six months. The ice floe kept drifting south and all the while it was getting smaller and smaller. Finally, the floe was only 50 sq.yds, and every time a

sea swept over it, a piece was washed away. At the end, they had to take to the boats and drift about in the ice pack in constant danger of being crushed. On April 28th they spotted a steamer. It disappeared, however, over the horizon. The same thing happened the next day, but on April 30th a ship appeared close by. It was a seal catcher from Newfoundland. The two Eskimos streaked along in their kayaks to enter the ship, and this time the shipwrecked were noticed. They were put ashore in St. Johns on May 13th.

The American government appointed a fact-finding committee, headed by officers of the Navy. But the whole affair was quickly covered up.

The rescue. The Scottish whaler RAVENSCRAIG *appears from the ice masses*

"We are Dying - like Men"

Had Lieutenant *Adolphis Washington Greely* of the United States cavalry made camp 25 miles further east than he did, he would probably not have become world famous. Furthermore, his shipmates would not have been forced to eat each other.

Greely's camp was located in the Ellesmere Island area, close to one of the richest hunting grounds in Northern Greenland, but this he did not know. In the course of nine months fourteen men starved to death. Of the 26 men in the expedition only seven survived.

Greeley's expedition was one of America's contributions to the First International Polar Year (1881).

Greely established an observatory, Fort Conger, in Lady Franklin Bay and stayed there until August of 1883. The idea was, the station should be visited once a year by a relief expedition and the crew replaced. But the relieving forces failed to appear in 1882 as well as in 1883. In 1883, one of the vessels with provisions, the PROTEUS, was crushed and sank in the ice. When the ship had disappeared, the crew thought they were no longer under orders and they refused to bring the provisions, which they had saved from the ship, on shore.

Out of the 50,000 rations which the relief expeditions had carried up along the coast of Greenland through Smith Sound, only 1000 were placed in caches. The rest was brought back to the States, or went down with the PROTEUS or was stolen.

In August 1883, Greely could no longer wait for the relief expedition. In four boats he and his men sailed down through Kane Basin all the while searching in vain for caches or relief expeditions. On the way he lost two boats, and turned north again along the coast of Ellesmere Island. Had he instead sailed across to the nearby Greenland coast, he would not only have found Eskimos who could help him, but also plenty of provisions.

He chose to make camp on Brevoort Island, a desolate, windswept island where he discovered the disheartening account of the loss of the PROTEUS. And here, on this spot, he inscribed his martyrdom in the history of arctic exploration.

In a stone house, using their last boat as a roof, his expedition spent a horrible winter of starvation. They caught only a few seals, a small bear, several foxes and a sort of sand-hopper, which they called shrimp. All leather was removed from shoes and clothing to be used for food, and the leather straps were boiled so that they could swallow them. In all, nineteen men lost their lives. 14 of them simply starved to death. One man died from scurvy. Sergeant Elison died from frost-bites. He lived for seven months with frost-bitten hands, feet and nose, suffering incredibly. In order to be able to guide the spoon to his mouth, he finally had it bound to what was left of his arm. One died of cold and exhaustion during a fishing trip and one, Private Henry, was executed by order of Greely. His crime was that he had stolen from the mutual supply of shoe laces, etc., which they used for boiling soup.

Lieutenant Lockwood died from starvation on April 9th, but right up until April 7th he had kept his diary and noted the barometer and thermometer readings.

In 1884 a rescue expedition of three ships, headed by Commander Winfield Scott Schley passed up through the water between Ellesmere Island and Greenland. On the way they laid out caches and by a stroke of luck they found a report from Greely. The message said that the expedition was fine and still had 40 rations left. The wonderful news was passed between the ships, but when they were through reading Greely's report, they met with a great disappointment. On the last page was printed the date: October 21st, 1883 –it was eight months since they had 40 rations left.

Deeply worried they continue north and finally spot a figure on a mountain. They signal, and the figure falls down twice. When they reach the place, they see a ghost before their eyes, with hollow cheeks, burning eyes, wispy hair

and a beard. Lieutenant Colwell from the relief expedition runs over to the nearest ţent. Close to the door lies a man who looks as if he is dead, with a hanging jaw and open, staring eyes. On the opposite side is a man with no hands and feet and with a spoon tied to his right arm stump. In front of the two, half sitting, half lying, is yet another man, dark haired with a long beard and strange, blazing eyes. He is wearing a small red skullcap on his head. When he sees the lieutenant, he draws himself up a little and puts on his spectacles. Colwell grasps his hand and asks if he is Greely. "Yes", he croaks, "seven of us are left. We are dying–like men. I have completed my task."

When preparing the dead bodies with alcohol, in order to be able to preserve them for the home voyage, it was discovered that big pieces of meat had been cut from some of them. Naval Com-

At long last the relief expedition arrives. Greely was just as unrecognizable as the six others. They had to say their names

mander Schley says in his report, "If that story ever has to be told it should come from the survivors themselves."

Greely nevertheless became a very old man. He died in 1925, 92 years old. 115

More and more scientists were interested in the inland ice, the icy wastes. Did any form of life exist there? In 1878 the Dane,
J. A. D. Jensen, ascended the ice cap at Frederikshaab and found a lot of ice free massifs thrusting through the ice. These are now
known as Jensen's Nunatakker. In 1883 the Swede, A. E. Nordenskiöld, pushed further onto the ice with his Lap skiers, but they, too,
had to turn back. The drawing made by Sv. Berggren gives a very precise picture of the dead icy wastes

The Inland Ice was Bad - but the Toasts were even Worse

The cheese, where's the cheese? The only piece of Swiss cheese on the ice cap had been left half a day's march behind. It had to be fetched. And it was. Dietrichson volunteered. He liked a little morning trip, he said, and then he walked the dangerous, icy and slippery route back to the spot where they had camped the day before.

This was August 16th 1888. The previous day Fridtjof Nansen, the prominent Norwegian scientist and arctic explorer, had begun his struggle against the inland ice of Greenland, which was to gain him world fame.

Others had tried to walk across the ice cap, but none had come very far before they had to turn back. What lay hidden behind these enormous ice masses which in some places rose to an elevation of 10,000 feet? A mild oasis? This was one of the theories, because sometimes warm Foehn winds spring up on the ice, causing fantastic fluctuations in temperatures along the coast.

Now Nansen wanted to learn the truth. The experts warned him. A Danish newspaper wrote: "Even though Nansen might be as mad as to try such a thing, he will not get one single person to join him, and alone he cannot make it."

Nevertheless, several hundred adventurous souls from all over the world came forward, and Nansen took the following five with him: E. C. Dietrichson, captain in the Norwegian army, 32 years, Otto Sverdrup, shipmaster, 33 years, Kristian Trana, a lumberjack, 24 years plus two Laps from the Finmark, Samuel Balto, 27 years and Ole Ravna, 45 years.

On July 17th, 1888 they were put out in boats from the seal catcher JASON into the field ice off Cape Dan. They intended to push through the field ice towards land and from there walk across the ice cap to Christianshaab in Western Greenland. Everything turned out quite different. The first 11 days they drifted south in the ice floes, until they came through the field ice and reached the coast 250 miles too far south.

Stubbornly they rowed north, approx. 200 miles, and only then did they start the difficult ascent to the inland ice.

Earlier they had pulled their boats across the sea ice from one hole to the

Departure in the morning on top of the inland ice

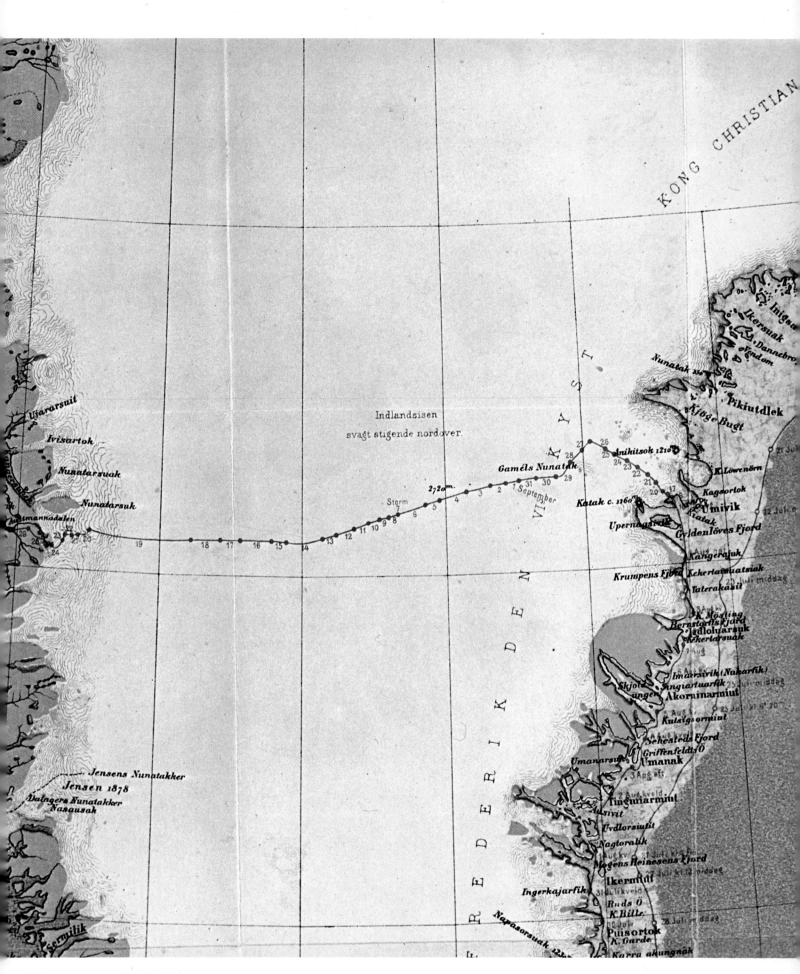

The route across the inland ice from Eastern to Western Greenland

next and now they pulled the heavy 100 pound sleds, two men to each sled, from crevasse to crevasse across the gnarled inland ice.

It turned out to be a 40-day walk through the icy wastes, in storm, frost and rain. They were plagued mostly by thirst, firewood for melting the ice being very scarce.

When they rested in the tent or rode out a storm, which could last up to three days, they slept or read the very few books they had.

Some distance inland they changed course. Nansen realized that he would not be able to reach Christianshaab in time to catch the last ship for Denmark that year, and furthermore they had a headwind. He decided to walk toward Godthaab, much farther to the south, and in doing so he had such favorable winds that he could set sails on the sleds. For a while the voyage went swimmingly.

When they approached the west coast and began the descent, they again faced difficulties. Here, the inland ice is intersected by deep crevasses. Nansen fell through the loose snow, but fortunately his stick got wedged across the crevasse and there he hung. The others were nowhere near him, but he succeeded in getting himself back on the solid ice again.

On September 26th the inland ice had been conquered. Below them lay the Austmanna Valley, a branch off the Ameralik Fjord, east-southeast of Godthaab. They were happy—and dirty. During their 40-day trip they had not washed one single time—and it suited them fine, Nansen declared afterwards.

Now the problem was to get help from Godthaab, but this, too, Nansen had anticipated. From the sleds and some sail cloth they made a very primitive boat which carried Nansen and Sverdrup to Godthaab. However, the

Fridtjof Nansen in great danger. Luckily his stick wedged itself across the crevasse

Nansen was honored by the Royal Danish Geographical Society at a ceremony in Copenhagen. Gentlemen covered with decorations and their ladies in beautiful dresses listened to his account of the trip across the inland ice

Nansen and Sverdrup in their self-made "boat", tied together with left-overs from the sleds, on their way to Godthaab

last ship had already left. Instead they spent a very gay winter in Greenland with plenty of parties and hunting trips.

On May 21st, 1889 the ship HVID-BJÖRNEN brought the expedition to Copenhagen, back to world fame and the many toasts. Later Nansen wrote in his account of the expedition, "Getting across Greenland was a tough job, but believe me, it was almost worse coming back."

121

The Road to the North Pole
Studded with Bear and Walrus

Nansen's next goal after the feat on the ice cap was reaching the North Pole. But he wanted to get there in an unorthodox way, namely letting himself drift over it. Along the east coast of Greenland driftwood from the Siberian forests had been found, which proved that a current must go across the North Pole and then south. In 1884 some Greenlanders from Julianehaab found a list of provisions, signed De Long, on an ice floe. He was a lieutenant in the American Navy, who shipwrecked with his ship JEANETTE at Wrangles Island on the other side of the North Pole, after having drifted with the ice for two years. By accident Nansen read about the discovery in a newspaper and decided to put the theory to a test.

In 1893, after having raised 444,000 Danish kr., Nansen's specially built ship FRAM was ready. It was fitted with an ice-sheathing of heavy planks, 25-35 inches thick and with sloping sides so that the pressure ice would press the ship up onto the ice instead of crushing it. Equipped with special provisions, rich in vitamins, and to last them five years, FRAM sailed from Norway in 1893. There were 13 persons aboard and at the table. Nansen certainly did not suffer from superstition. To this he added 34 dogs which he picked up in Northern Siberia.

FRAM entered the ice pack near the New Siberian Islands and started to drift towards the North Pole. Nansen's theory proved to be right. But after a year and a half of drifting he realized that the ship would not get close enough to the North Pole.

All right: the North Pole would not come to Nansen, then he would come to the North Pole.

Together with Lieutenant Hjalmar

122   The crew on FRAM. *Nansen is sitting, wearing a flat-crowned hat, behind the man with the dog*

FRAM *in the fantastic pack ice. The special construction of the ship had the effect that the ice was unable to "bite" into the ship, but pushed it upwards instead of pressing it down*

The incredible walk toward the North Pole. Nansen had to give up only 270 miles from his mark

Johansen, who was also a meteorologist, he left the rest of the crew to conquer the North Pole, taking a total of 28 dogs, two boats and three sleds. We will be back in civilization in five months, they declared, but it took them almost one year. After having dragged themselves across the ice pack all the way up to 86° 14', they had to give up only 270 miles from the North Pole.

They had begun to starve and therefore they headed south towards Franz Joseph's Land where they built a hut for the winter. Here was plenty of game. Fights with bears and walruses was the order of the day. On one occasion they had a very near escape. Nansen was attacked by a walrus who popped up close to his boat and dug its tusks into the side of it. He escaped from the sinking vessel onto an ice floe where Johansen too had sought refuge.

It was spring of 1896 and something wonderful happened. Just like Stanley met Livingstone in the jungles of Africa, Nansen met Frederick G. Jackson in this, the most godforsaken spot on earth.

During a skiing trip on the sea ice, Nansen suddenly heard the howling of a dog. And from behind the pressure ice a man, dressed in impeccable British tailor-made clothes, shaven and well-groomed, suddenly appeared. There stood Nansen, dirty, unshaven and almost in rags. They greeted each other with a "How do you do?" and walked together a little without saying anything. Suddenly the Englishman said, "Say, you're not Mr. Nansen, are you?"

Nansen and Johansen returned to Norway on August 13th 1896 on board Jackson's ship, the same day that FRAM finally got free of the ice at Spitsbergen.

Nansen and Johansen tied the two boats together and sailed across every time they came upon open water

Drawing of Nansen's fight with a walrus which dug its tusks into his boat and nearly was the death of him

"How do you do?" The famous meeting between Nansen and Jackson in 1896

A Swedish Tragedy - and a Norwegian Triumph

At the beginning of the 20th century no one had yet reached the North Pole and no one had yet sailed through the Northwest Passage. The latter had long ago lost any practical importance as a sailing route to China and India. The North Pole and the Passage were only viewed as sporting or scientific objects. This, however, did not prevent people from trying.

In 1897 the Swedes S. A. Andreé, Nils Strindberg and Knut Fränkel tried to fly to the North Pole in the balloon ÖRNEN. They started out from Spitsbergen. The conclusion came 33 years later, when their bodies, some film and their diaries were found in a tent on White Island north of Spitsbergen. During all these years their disappearance had been a mystery. The diaries disclosed that they had landed on an ice floe at 83° N. and had to walk across the ice to White Island, where they died in their tent. They only had one sleeping bag to share between them.

The young Norwegian arctic explorer Roald Amundsen had better luck in his venture. He aimed at the Northwest Passage, and this decision he took when he was a small boy, watching Nansen return from his walk across the inland ice. "Just think, if I could do the Northwest Passage," he said himself in the midst of the cheering crowd. In 1903 he set course north in the ship GJÖA.

At Cape York he spotted two Eski-

On July 14th 1897 Andreé and his men had to land their balloon on the ice after 65 hours in the air. His dreams did not come true

mos streaking toward the ship in two kayaks. He was rather surprised to see that one was decorated with a Norwegian flag, the other with a Danish. Then the two kayak men came aboard and introduced themselves: Mylius-Erichsen and Knud Rasmussen. On his way towards world fame, Amundsen had met two of the participants in the Danish Literary Greenland Expedition which too, was on its way into the history of arctic exploration.

GJÖA continued towards the Northwest Passage along Franklin's old route. After having wintered three times the small craft finally pushed its way through the ice masses. On the way, Amundsen and his companions had found skeletons of Franklin's men and built cairns over them. On the magnetic North Pole they had made valuable observations. The crew who sailed through the Northwest Passage consisted of only six men.

GJÖA *wintering in the ice*

The North Pole Did Not Have Room for Two

The wast ice masses of the North Pole did not have room for two equally ambitious men. This became apparent from the bitter quarrel arising between Frederick A. Cook and Robert E. Peary, when each of them claimed to have attained his life's ambition. That Peary was the discoverer of the North Pole is considered an indisputable fact today. In 1909, however, when he announced from a radio station in Labrador that he had been at the North Pole, he was not believed by very many. The world simply did not feel like celebrating two men for the same feat, and in April of that same year Cook, together with two Eskimos, claimed to have been there ahead of Peary.

When in September 1909 Cook arrived in Copenhagen directly from the Arctic Regions, everybody paid homage to him. Great crowds were waiting at the quay. He was received by the Danish crown prince, the American ambassador and representatives of scientific societies who wished to congratulate him. Later, many honors were bestowed on him and he was given several decorations. At the beginning the press was rather sceptical, but the journalists who came aboard the ship which brought Cook back, sent reports home, telling of "his strange shy and kind smile, his trustworthy blue eyes, his rather pointed nose (from hunger), his shabby looking clothes and his stocky, quiet person."

Peary, on the other hand, had a rather chilly reception, and thus began a year-long dispute which ended with Cook being marked as a swindler. For one thing, because of a an ex-captain who claimed that Cook on some hotel room had asked him to work out a series of North Pole reckonings, which were to

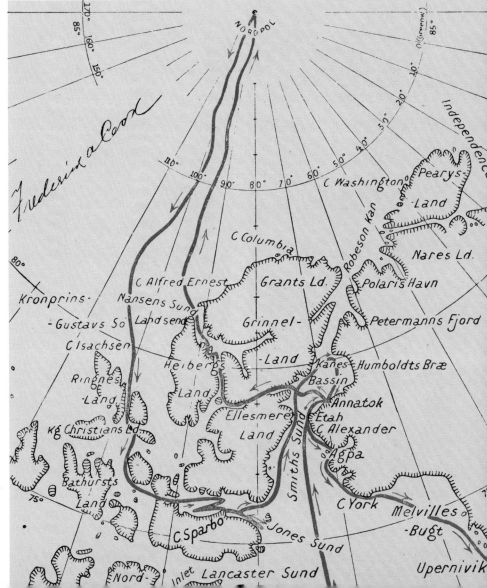

Dr. Cook's route to and from the North Pole

From the banquet held in Cook's honor by the Copenhagen daily "Politiken". Cook is wearing a wreath of flowers around his neck. The people in the photo look taken aback. The reason: they have just heard a telegram announcing that Peary has discovered the North Pole

prove to the University of Copenhagen that Cook really had been at the North Pole. The price of these rekonings was 2500 dollars and an additional 1500 dollars if Copenhagen believed in them. "The New York Times" published the story, which Cook immediately denied. Only much later was Peary officially recognized as the discoverer of the North Pole.

Peary's expedition was gigantic. Three years earlier, also on his way to the North Pole, he had to turn back for lack provisions. He did not want this to happen again. His ship the ROOSEVELT was especially designed for arctic conditions and he took with him 49 arctic Eskimos, 246 dogs and three tons

of feed. In 1905 he sailed north, all the way up to 82° 30' through the Kennedy Channel.

Here the expedition was divided into parties, all following the same route north. Peary with his men brought up the rear. Caches were laid out along the way and thus he built a sort of bridge to the North Pole. Peary, his servant, the negro Matthew Henson and four Eskimos made the final push and reached the Pole on April 6th 1909. He stayed in the area for 30 hours. When he returned to the ROOSEVELT he was received with the sad news that one of the members of the expedition, professor Ross G. Marvin, had been drowned in an ice lane.

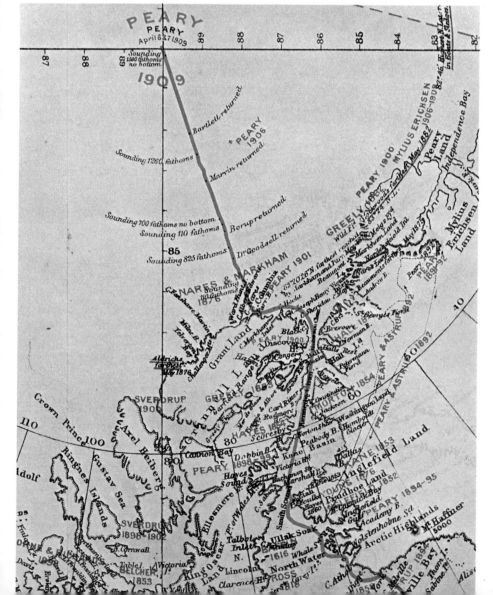

Professor Ross G. Marvin.
Was he murdered?

Peary's route to the North Pole

Cook's picture which he claimed had been taken at the North Pole

Wherever Peary came he built cairns with accounts of his push towards the Pole. This cairn was found many years later —containing a whiskey bottle with an account written by Peary. The cross with the letter "R" stands for the ship ROOSEVELT

The picture taken of the victorious Peary was rather more stately than the picture taken of Cook. There is no doubt that it was photographed at the North Pole, but it could be anywhere in Greenland

There is every probability, however, that Marvin was murdered.

One of Marvin's two companions, by Peary called Kud-Look-Too, has been mentioned as the alleged murderer by the Eskimos. The deed had only one witness, the Eskimo Harrigan. Some years ago, he told his story once more to a Danish radio reporter. "Marvin had bawled us out, and we had been rather gloomy during the entire trip, because we had discovered that he had eaten from our daily rations behind our backs. When we came to some pack ice, Marvin and Kud-Look-Too went up to the top. Suddenly Kud-Look-To cried out that he had seen a seal and that I should bring the rifle.

I brought the rifle. Marvin stood a few paces away from us. Suddenly Kud-Look-Too cried: 'Look at the seal down there!' Marvin turned around and at that moment Kud-Look-Too shot the American."

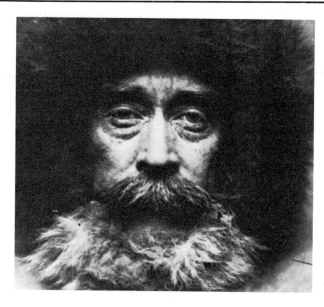

A tired man who had attained his life's ambition

Robert E. Peary was 52 years of age when he reached the North Pole. A high age for an active arctic explorer. He was educated as a civil engineer, but most of his life was spent working for his great goal: reaching the North Pole. His first voyage to Northern Greenland took place in 1886 when, together with the Danish trading assistant Christian Maigaard, he walked onto the inland ice north of Jakobshavn. They reached 120 miles inland before they had to turn back. For Peary this was a sort of trial run. He was not interested in the inland ice.

His next big voyage took place in 1892, when, together with a Norwegian, Eivind Astrup, he walked across the northern part of the ice cap from Inglefield Bay to Navy Cliff at the bottom of Independence Fjord. He was the first to confirm Greenland's insular character. During the following years he made numerous journeys to Northern Greenland.

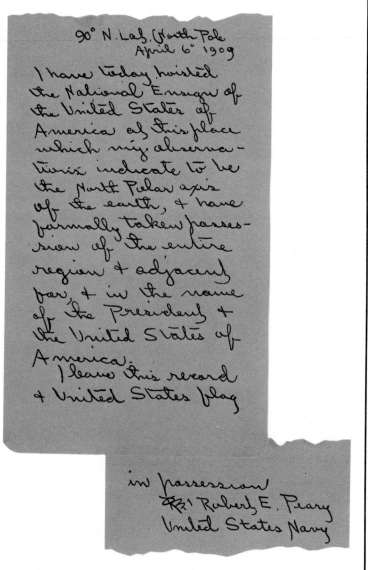

Peary's famous announcement in which he claims that he has reached the North Pole and that he has taken possession of it in the name of the American President

131

When the Danes finally got their Kamiks off the Ground

The big foreign expeditions to or via Greenland had very ambitious aims which were not, however, of any immediate importance to the Greenlanders. It was quite different with the many Danish expeditions, even though these started comparatively late.

Like the Greenlanders, the Danes were rather like spectators of the international activity in the Arctic Regions. It is true that in 1829 a Danish naval lieutenant W. A. Graah had been sent on an expeditionary voyage to Eastern Greenland in order to find the Eastern Settlement of the Norsemen, but half a century was to pass before the Danes got their kamiks off the ground.

The turning point was 1878. At that time the government appointed a "Committee for the Direction of Geological and Geographical Research in Greenland". Over the years this committee sent out a great number of expeditions, the results of which were published in the huge 60-volume works, "Meddelelser om Grönland" (Accounts of Greenland).

In the wake of these expeditions, Danish names began to turn up on the map of Greenland. The first aim was the exploration of Eastern Greenland, then followed Northern Greenland and Northeast Greenland. Many of the voyages took place in rather primitive circumstances, often at the risk of the explorers' lives. Some never returned, but actually, the losses were surprisingly few and small when you consider the terrible hardships and dangers to which the explorers exposed themselves.

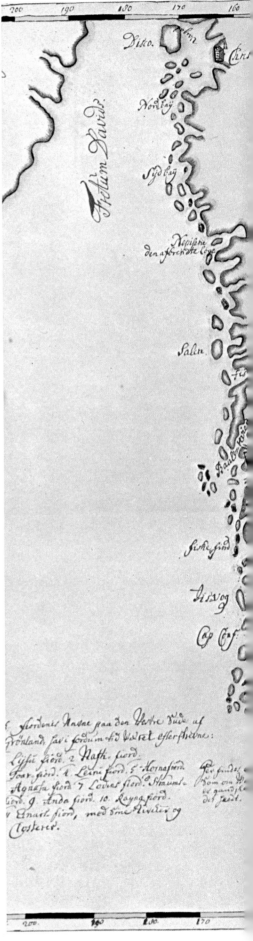

A storm coming up over the unexplored Eastern Greenland

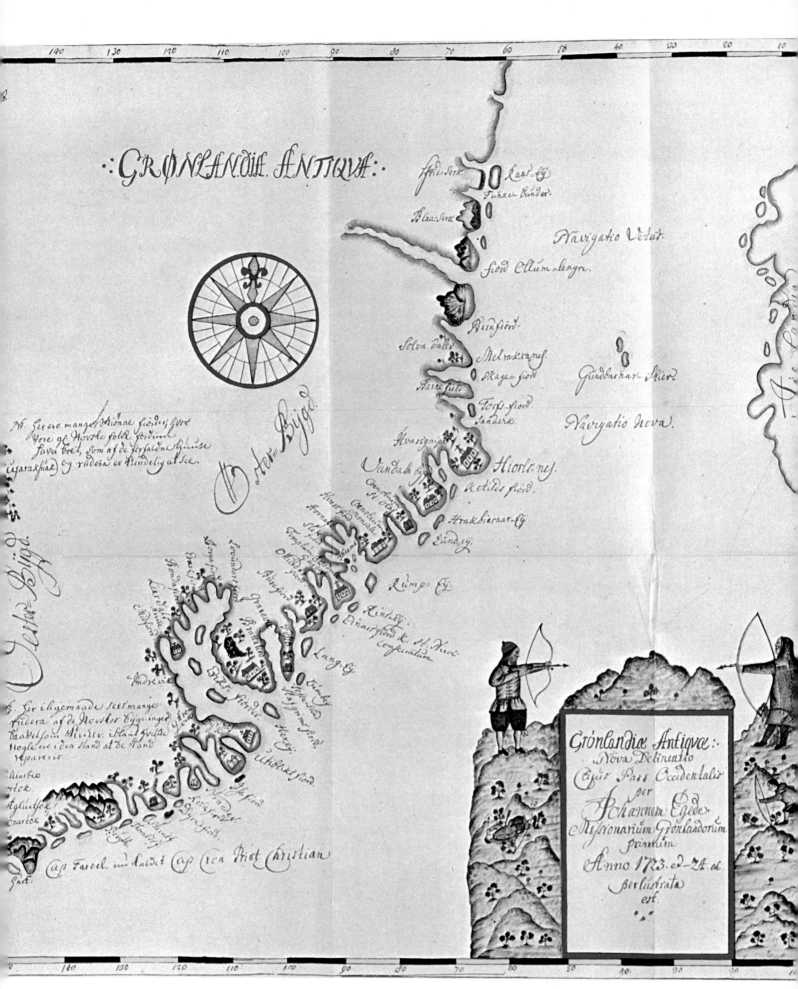

This is how Hans Egede's map looked. He thought that the Eastern Settlement was to be found in Eastern Greenland

To the Land where Women are Slaughtered

With a sour-looking Black Dorte as the boatswain, a peculiar procession started out from Nanortalik on March 21st, 1829. This famed Exploration-Voyage to the east coast of Greenland consisted of four Danes, five Greenlanders, ten Greenland women in an umiak, followed by a heavily laden transport vessel and surrounded by a swarm of kayaks. Lieutenant Commander Graah had royal orders to find surviving descendants of the Norsemen and the Eastern Settlement which Hans Egede before him had sought in vain. Graah was happy that the journey had finally started after one whole year's preparations. But Black Dorte was equally sulky because she had been chosen for their boatswain. Her task was to be ready with the sewing needle in case the skin of the umiak was damaged.

On May 23rd Graah met the first Eastern Greenlanders, two families in a tent. "The two Women did not have the Greenland Physiognomy at all, and their entire Appearance was strangely different from that of the Greenland Women on the West Coast: They did not have the fleshy Bodies or the prominent Bellies; they were both above Middle Height and remarkable for their regular, beautiful facial Features, their clear Complexion and the oval Form of their Heads." Graah praised their cleanliness and beautiful clothes at the expense of the ladies on the west coast who "most certainly spruce themselves up on the Holidays with Ribbons and Pearls and gaily coloured Skins, but show themselves all the more filthy the Rest of the Week."

On June 20th Graah did not dare to go any further north with his big expedition. He decided to continue alone, accompanied only by the great hunter Erneneq and his two wives. Furthermore, two old women from Nanortalik volunteered. They allowed themselves to be persuaded by the many pearls and other finery which Graah laid before them. Also, he continued, "because they expected to find more truthful Lovers on the East Coast than they had found at Home. It was rumoured that the Eastern Greenlanders had the horrible Habit of slaughtering their Women, when they experienced a Famine, wherefore the Women usually had three or four Men."

Graah continued north on June 23rd, while the others started back. On October 1st the expedition took winter cover. Near Nuqarbiq Graah built a twelve feet long peat hut where he wintered together with Black Dorte and another of the women rowers who had found herself a lover in the necromancer Ningeoaq. His job consisted mostly of singing and chanting sermons, which he had learned by heart, for the Greenlanders. When he forgot the rest of the sermon "he started counting in German."

In the spring Graah went north again to the vicinity of Angmagssalik, but his rowers wanted to get back home and he realized that if he stayed one more winter, he would die from hunger. They turned back south and after numerous difficulties he reached the colony of the Moravian Brethren, Friedrichsthal, on October 16th. He stayed the winter in Southern Greenland, and on September 13th 1831 he once more saw Kronborg. The outcome of the expedition? Aside from the mapping, etc. his own conclusion was: "The Eastern Settlement is the District of Julianehaab. The East Coast of Greenland has never had a Colony."

The family pattern in Eastern Greenland, Graah wrote, is rather simple. If a man wants a bride, he just takes her and does not pay any attention to the question of a dowry. And if a man wants to get rid of his wife, all he has to do is acting grumpy and leaving his house for a few days without telling where he is. "Then right away she knows what is what; she packs her Clothes, takes the Children and moves back to her Family and Friends."

The girls do nothing until they are 12 or 13 years of age, except play, fetch water and babysit. Later on they have to sew, cook, slaughter, tan, row the umiak, build houses and catch sharks, "the latter being the Women's favourite Pastime on moonlit Winter Nights."

Graah himself once saw how a man took a bride. A young man, whom Graah did not like, started to drag off one of Graah's young rowers. She yelled and screamed, while the other Greenlanders watched passively. In the end Graah had to come to the rescue of the girl. He was under the impression that she did not at all wish to be married to the young man. But when Graah broke camp, the woman disappeared in search of her suitor. It was customary to resist.

Performing the drum dance in Graah's winter hut. Black Dorte is sulking on the bed. She had no lover

Old drawing of an umiak. Apparently, the weather is not all that cold in Greenland

On Their Way to the Wild Heathens

It took more than half a century before the Danes once more explored Eastern Greenland. In May of 1884 "The Danish Umiak Expedition" sailed from Nanortalik in four umiaks and seven kayaks. The ambition was to continue where Graah had left off. The leader was Lieutenant G. F. Holm with Lieutenant T. V. Garde as second in command. A total of 37 persons participated in the expedition. Two brothers of Danish -Greenland extraction, Hendrik and Johan Petersen served as interpreters, their services proving very valuable to later expeditions.

The two Danish naval lieutenants who became respectively Commander and Admiral, had acclimatized themselves in Southern Greenland. After a description of the inhuman conditions under which the Greenlanders live in their earthen huts, they wrote: "When you gather all these Impressions–the small, damp Earth Huts in which many People live without Ventilation, without Cleanliness and very often without proper Bed Linen, one might think that the Greenland Houses were of such a Nature that we Europeans were able to enter into them only with the utmost Disgust. But the Kindness and good Manners of the People are a great Help.

When you have lived in Greenland for some Time and have come to know the Inhabitants, you feel a Desire to associate more with them. You forget all Prejudice, your Eyes do not see the Dirt but rest on the bright, lively Faces, and even though the Coffee Cup is cleaned with a not so clean Thumb, the Coffee tastes quite good. How often have we not at Christmas Time or on some other special Occasion had the most happy Moments in the small Greenland huts. Even one of the Trading Company's cheap Cigars tasted quite agreeable when smoked in the House of a Greenlander."

The Danish expeditions were not only of scientific importance. Their accounts of the conditions in Greenland opened the eyes of the public back in Denmark to absurdities which ought to be corrected. Among other things, Holm and Garde described the so-called hunger period in Southern Greenland. At periods a dozen starved wretches stood outside their door in the morning, begging for a little bread or a little money to buy rye flour. Each beggar represented a family of several equally hungry members.

A very important member of the expedition was the Greenland catechist, Johannes Hansen, called Hanseraq. He, so he said, was going to preach the Word to these ungodly heathens on the east coast. At Inugsuit, where they met the first big crowd of heathens, Hanseraq stood up on a big stone and like a true apostle began preaching the Gospel. Holm and Garde demonstrated that the Eastern Greenlanders did not understand much of all his talk, mostly because Hanseraq was unable to explain clearly to them what it was all about. When he suggested that they move to the missions in Western Greenland, the two Danes had to interfere. They had seen all too often what happened to the Eastern Greenlanders when they fell into temptation at the trading station. Either they were destroyed or they became poor and unhappy.

"One of the worst Mistakes on the West Coast, aside from the unlimited Trade, is that all the Greenlanders' good old traditional Customs and their Conceptions of Justice have been forbidden, without giving them a Form of Compensation, just because they are 'Heathens.' Holm and Garde continue: "The People have been declared incapable of Managing their own Affairs, they are dependent on the Danish Missionaries and Policemen."

*Greenlanders in front of peat hut 1884.
It is easily understandable why the two
Danish lieutenants were very concerned
with the conditions under which the
Greenlanders lived*

*Hanseráq who spoke warningly to the
wild heathens, was later decorated for his
services*

The umiak expedition divided at
Tingmiarmit. Most of them turned back
to continue the exploration of the southern coast, while the rest, under the
command of Holm, continued north to
winter at Angmagssalik, where they
were in close contact with "the heathens".

Holm visited a big family house with
about fifty inhabitants. "A Lot of naked
People were seen everywhere, lying on
the Bed, tossing and cuddling and
caressing each other like Dogs.

In General, the People were beautiful
and well-formed, but watching the old
Women with their hanging Breasts and
the Women in an advanced Stage of
Pregnancy was a less attractive Sight."

During the visit they served half
-rotten seal, which they ate uncommonly
quickly. The rotten meat and the entrails emitted an unbelievable stench,
but everything was eaten with gluttony.

One day Holm was visited by a great
number of men who told him that Piti-
ka's wife would give birth to a son.
They were convinced that it would be
a son, because angekokken, the necromancer, had said so. To this end the
expectant father had ordered his wife
to wear several amulets. Nevertheless,
the baby was a girl.

137

Holm also writes that the Eastern Greenlander actually is very kind to his wife, when she becomes pregnant. Immediately she has his best attention. When the child is born, it is washed off in the urinal bucket, whereafter the mother strokes it on the mouth with a finger dipped in water. At the same time she repeats the names of the dead after which the child is to be named. Above all the child will have the name of the person who has died last, because the Greenlanders believe that the name stays with the dead body, until a child is named after it and can continue life.

Children who are born weak or whose mother dies during birth, are thrown outside on the ground or in the ocean. Children, who are put to death in this manner, "arc going to Heaven where they make the Northern Lights". The light is produced when the children play ball, especially with the afterbirth. After the birth, the entire house is cleaned, including the walls and the furs and skins from the bed. Even the casings for the windows are washed.

The children are breast-fed until they are two years old. All their games have to do with hunting and rowing umiaks or kayaks. The children learn to be proficient in making miniature hunting tools. They practice shooting at sparrows with small bows or darts. For the girls there are dolls made of wood and rattles made of bear teeth. The children walk about the house completely naked until they are 16 years of age. Then they start wearing small skin briefs, which they call "natit". As soon as a boy starts wearing natit, the girls begin to smile at him, and then he is marriageable. The girls wear their hair down their back until they start wearing natit. Then the hair is arranged in a top knot, and they are marriageable, too. The marriage takes place without special ceremony. The girl must be taken forcibly and must be "abducted". All this takes place with much yelling and screaming. Holm mentions that abduction of other men's wives also happens. The man who wishes to kidnap a woman, takes along an empty kayak, he fetches the desired woman from 'her tent and tries to get her into the kayak. Then the whole thing is over, unless it turns out that the husband is stronger than the abductor. Some men have two wives, but usually live very peacefully with both. It happens that one of them gets a black eye or is "restrained" with a knife in her thighs or arms, "but soon their relations are as affectionate as before."

Dokoda was unimpressed when, in 1900, he came aboard a ship for the first time

A couple from Angmagssalik in front of a summer tent

Primitive People with Bowler Hats and Standard Shirts

Ten years after his umiak expedition in 1896, Gustav Holm returned to Angmagssalik as commander of the steamship HVIDBJÖRNEN and he founded the colony which kept the name Angmagssalik. Johan Petersen who had served him earlier as an interpreter was made colony manager, and pastor P. Rüttel became the colony pastor and missionary.

The previous two years had seen famine in Eastern Greenland. The population figure for Angmagssalik had dropped from 413 to 247. Some of the dead had been eaten up by the others.

The Eastern Greenlanders had already had contact with civilization in the form of a Norwegian ship which had been forced to winter in the ice.

Pastor Rüttel almost cried when he went ashore. What a reception! "One is wearing a Silk Hat, another Knee Breeches, Stockings and Shoes so that you should think he was going to the Court of the German Emperor. One is acting the Gentleman in a Frock Coat, another is wearing a Standard Shirt and almost nothing else."

The Norwegians had grossly exploited the Greenlanders. They had received a lot of skins in return for a few old rifles, some ammunition and various old rags.

Pastor Rüttel stayed with the heathens for ten years. It is evident from his diary that he was plagued more by murderers than by necromancers. It did not do much good that he and the colony manager announced that they would not trade with people committing murder. And the pastor was completely heart-broken when receiving a letter from a colleague in Nanortalik. In the letter the missionary told about an Eastern Greenlander, who was wintering there, and who had notified him that

Angmagssalik at the turn of the century. Aside from the rogue at the back, all have serious, heavy faces

Brides and grooms from Angmagssalik, anno 1900. At that time kamiks and bowler hats seemed to be the fashion in wedding wear

he wanted to travel back to Angmagssalik next year, because there were three people, whom he wished to kill.

The situation was in fact very serious. Murders and blood feuds were the order of the day, and as a rule, the victims were always the capable hunters. During the fall, before the pastor arrived, a whole string of murders took place. One man, who had himself murdered three people, was pulled out of his tent by three others, and while the two of them held him, the third murdered him with a knife. Then they dismembered the body and threw it into the water. On the spot

Polygamy was not easy to stamp out. Here Kunaq is entertaining his wives and children with the drum (1906)

where Gustav Holm had wintered, a murder happened during a drum dance. The man, who was murdered, was no murderer, but he was suspected of "stealing souls."

The pastor also had to struggle with suicides. On one occasion the colony manager found a woman on the edge of a rock with her clothes all wrapped up, ready to throw herself into the water. She explained that she was afraid of dying on land, beause then the dogs and ravens would eat her. No one wanted to bury her, because they thought she was a witch. The pastor was summoned and together the two men carried her back to the tent where she had lived. But the tent had been torn down. "It was no good that she would come out through the Tent Opening in her Shroud." And she could not be put back into her Tent, since she had already prepared herself to die. No one dared to touch her, except her small Daughter."

The pastor took her to his house, where she was allowed to die in a bed.

Pastor Rüttel also writes about murders of children. It is a tradition that women who become widows throw their small children into the water, because now they no longer have anyone to support them.

There is 60 years' difference between these two longhaired men. Kuitse, the bear killer, stepped right out of the stone age at the turn of the century, and his grandchild, Ulrik Kuitse, worker and pop musician, flew into the jet age 60 years later. In Sdr. Strømfjord a Danish journalist met him just as he was going by DC-8 to Denmark. The grandfather's scar on the chest was caused by a bear which crushed his kayak and bit him while he was still under water

It did not always take a murder to settle grievances though. Most disputes were settled with satirical songs. During the bright summer the people gathered at specific spots and often travelled from far away to attend these gatherings.

The opponents made the most terrible songs about each other, so that they were made to look ridiculous in the eyes of the spectators. The great thing was to find as many dirty words and arguments as possible. The opponents knocked their skulls together or their noses–very often the result was a broken nose.

The drum dances and the satirical songs belong to the past, but there are still older Eastern Greenlanders, like the ones in the pictures here, who know this age-old art.

Modern courts and the world's most humane criminal law have replaced the satirical songs. Punitive measures as we know them from the Western world is very seldom used in Greenland. A murder, for instance, does not necessarily bring about the murderer's imprisonment. Maybe he will just be sentenced to move to another community to get an education which the court has judged might make him a better member of society.

These pictures, taken in Eastern Greenland in 1971, show the age-old art of drum dancing

A Race against Death

The Danish Literary Greenland Expedition began with a dance and finished with a race against death by sled through hitherto unexplored areas. The leader of the expedition was the Danish arctic explorer Ludvig Mylius-Erichsen. The other members of the expedition were the artist Harald Moltke, Dr. Alfred Berthelsen, the writer Knud Rasmussen, Jörgen Brönlund who was a catechist and two Greenland bear hunters, Adam and Markus.

At home, the expedition had had its difficulties with the authorities. Greenland was a closed country, especially for people who wrote, and Mylius-Erichsen worked for the Copenhagen daily, Politiken. But finally they succeeded in getting travel permission. The last evening before the long sled voyage, they held a big dance in Tassiussak just north of Upernavik. "It was so crowded in the small Room that no more than four Couples could dance on the Spot at one Time. The Temperature was Tropical." Mylius-Erichsen wrote later: "The Walls cried away their month-long icy cover."

During the voyage Moltke became ill. Brönlund and Knud Rasmussen were sent off to get some help, and Mylius-Erichsen was to follow them with the sick man. Moltke's illness left an indelible stamp on most of the expedition, because his condition got worse and worse. In the end, most of his body was paralyzed and he was in great pain. After a trip, on which Knud Rasmussen completely wore out one of his dogs, they succeeded in getting Moltke to more comfortable surroundings with an Eskimo family, and later in the winter he was brought back to Upernavik, where he slowly recovered.

Knud Rasmussen tells about his first meeting with the Cape York Eskimos—to whom he was to devote much of his life and who were to become his best friends

The main force of the Literary Greenland Expedition, photographed by Roald Amundsen on the GJÖA. The artist Harald Moltke is standing at the far left, behind him Knud Rasmussen and at the far right Mylius-Erichsen.
The young man between Knud Rasmussen and Mylius-Erichsen is probably Jörgen Brönlund. The Greenlander in the foreground is thought to be Gaba

—they gave him quite a fantastic reception. Immediately afterwards he made an ass of himself, when he, as was the custom in Western Greenland, put his feet out towards a young girl so that she could help him get his overboots off. She blushed, and the incident caused a great commotion. Not until later did Knud Rasmussen learn the reason: Actually he had proposed to the girl.

"SiTLO"
•AGPAT•1903
HMOLTKE

Harald Moltke's masterly drawing of a girl from Cape York

A Drum Song Fixed Peary

Typical Cape York Eskimo

The small Eskimo tribe, the most northerly in the world, consisted of 200 people, all strong and healthy, chosen by the rule of nature: survival of the fittest. Mylius-Erichsen and Knud Rasmussen noted that contact with European civilization had already made the Eskimos dependent on it. From Peary and the Scottish whalers they had learned to use the rifle, and if they did not get enough ammunition, they were badly off. It never dawned on them that the whalers or Peary might not return. "But Peary comes every year," they answered.

The hour-long winter conversations with the Eskimos revealed the mutual jealousy of the arctic explorers. Peary's best helpers, Marsanguark and Panigpark, told that Peary had forbidden them to have anything at all to do with the FRAM expedition. "The captain on the big white ship was Peary's worst enemy. Marré (Peary's servant, the negro Mathew Henson) had told them this, because the master of the big white ship had stolen papers from Peary–drawings of the countries hereabouts without which the master of the big white ship would not have been able to find his way up here. And here, Peary apparently wanted to be the only big master, who drew the countries."

Then the two snickering Eskimos told how it happened that Peary lost his toes. "We were going up to the house where Griwli (Greely), the one who lost so many of his men and who also ate the dead, had lived." It was in December and it took more mornings than the

Eskimos could count. Peary was unable to change kamiks often enough. "The inside skin was damp and more toes than I have dogs, maybe seven, were numb with cold." Finally, Peary had reached Griwli's house, but had to stay there because he was quite ill. He had suffered much up there, Sipsuk and the others said, and often he cried from the pain. When they came back to the ship with him, the sick toes were cut off with a pair of scissors. Marré has told that "the ship's doctor first killed Peary a little with some medicine, before he

Meeting in Melville Bay. When Eskimos meet, today as in Knud Rasmussen's time, they start their sweet palaver. The people from the south are wearing sealskin breeches, those from the north wear bearskin clothes. The equipment on the sleds, the provisions and the hunting gear has not changed

146

started to cut, and when Peary came back from the dead, he was without his seven toes."

They also recounted how the necromancer Angutigavsik had managed a brawl with Peary. The necromancer was driving sled provisions for Peary, and, in the end, when he was tired of slaving, he had thrown the provisions off his sled and turned tail back to the snow hut. Peary was furious, of course. He threatened the entire settlement and set off in pursuit of Angutigavsik. When he arrived at the snow hut, he viciously kicked at the wall of the hut, and when the necromancer did not come out, he tore the ice block away from the entrance. "Angutigavsik thought that Peary would shoot him when he crawled in and took his rifle away from him. But he told us later, that he was not at all afraid, because his only answer to Peary's furious words had been drum songs. Angutigavsik continued his drum songs and every time Peary found new words for his anger, the necromancer started on a new song. Finally, Peary had no choice but to calm down."

Knud Rasmussen in his element   147

The Northernmost Danish Outpost

Knud Rasmussen, Mylius-Erichsen and Moltke returned to Denmark with some fantastic tales and suggested to the Danish government that it annex the Cape York area. No one seemed interested, however, even though it was known that Americans, Germans and Norwegians had plans for establishing a trading station. In religious circles, however, it attracted attention that 200 heathens lived in Northern Greenland, and led by the Bishop of Zealand it was decided to raise a subscription for the establishing of a mission.

Knud Rasmussen had nothing to do with these plans. He had gone north again, first to Western Greenland, and when Melville Bay was covered with ice, he set out with loaded sleds for the

Knud Rasmussen among his Thule friends

Mother with children inside a tent 1909

Young mother from Cape York 1905

Cape York Eskimos. The whalers had not turned up and there was a shortage of almost everything, in particular of ammunition. Knud Rasmussen stayed with the Eskimos for two years, from the winter of 1906 to 1908. The following year he was asked to help in getting the mission station under way. It was established in 1909 and since the Danish government still did not take any action, he started the "Cape York Station Thule" at his own expense in 1910. This was primarily in order to secure Northern Greenland for Denmark, but also to raise money for the expeditions he had planned. Finally, it was the task of the station to provide the Eskimos with the things on which they had become dependent through bartering with the Scots whalers and the American expeditions.

On August 19th 1910 Knud Rasmussen hoisted the Danish flag over his small trading station. The year before it had floated over the mission and when Peary arrived on his last trip in 1909, he was so confused that he forgot to steer his ship. It ran aground—even though Peary was familiar enough with the local navigation conditions.

The manager of the station was Peter Freuchen. He became Knud Rasmussen's companion for life and his close friend. Freuchen was a giant of a man. As a popular writer of stories about the Eskimos' life and about arctic conditions he was second to none, but actually he started in a very humble arctic job. In 1906 Mylius-Erichsen hired the young medical student as a stoker on the ship which was to carry his planned expedition to Northeastern Greenland —an expedition which took such a tragic course.

Jesting and Joking in the Dark

Several years back a "summer man" (the name for Danes spending only a few summer months in Greenland) asked a Greenland acquaintance, "Well, how is the wife-swapping these days?" "You had better ask the Danes about that," was the Greenlander's reply.

The church and Danish morals had put a stop to both "Snuff the Lamp" games and wife-swapping. This you have to travel much farther south to experience.

About twenty years ago it was considered gross infidelity among the arctic Eskimos if a wife started to sew or repair something for another man. On the other hand everybody found it quite natural that she slept with some other man, that is, if her husband had consented to it.

Peter Freuchen, who lived for many years in Thule, maintains that wife-swapping was done for practical reasons, too. When on a hunting trip it was absolutely necessary for the men to have a woman along–to cook, warm up the snow hut and prepare the skins which they brought home. If their own wife was prevented from going–she might be in an advanced stage of pregnancy or ill–then they took along the wife of another hunter, who would not be going. And on the long trips an intimate relationship was inevitable. Peter Freuchen tells how he himself borrowed a young, beautiful wife. She had developed a taste for white men while on board one of Peary's ships, and her husband thought that maybe she would work it off with Peter Freuchen. They were away for several months, but as soon as they returned to the settlement, she did not as much as send Freuchen a look, but went straight to her husband as if she had only been away a short time.

Sometimes wife-swapping took place just for the fun of it. During a short hunting trip the men sometimes agreed to visit each other's wives the following night, and they thought it great fun to keep the plan a secret from their wives, until they walked out of their own house and into someone else's when it was time to go to bed. The necromancer could order an exchange of wives, too, if the hunting failed and he had to pacify the "big woman at the bottom of the sea who sends out the animals to feed the people." Angakokken decided what woman should sleep with what man, and if the hunters had not caught anything within a few days, he tried a new combination, until all the men had visited all the women in the settlement. After that he had to resort to other measures.

Peter Freuchen was born on one of the islands south of Zealand and subscribed to the local newspaper while living in Greenland. He received the numbers for an entire year at a time, but only read one every day. When living in Thule is does not matter if the news is a year old

Peter Freuchen writes that the rules for "Snuff the Lamp" games were very simple. A lot of people were gathered completely naked in one of the houses. Then the lamps were snuffed out so that it was pitchdark. No one was allowed to say anything and everybody kept changing places. At a certain signal each man grabbed the nearest woman. After some time the lamps were lit again, and many witty remarks exchanged, such as: "I knew all the time who it was, because . . ."

"Snuff the Lamp" was also a psychological game, especially if a group of Eskimos were weather-bound somewhere. This could be a strain on everybody's nerves.

Suddenly somebody snuffs out the lamp, there is a lot of running around in the dark and finally everybody has found a companion.

Later the lamp is lit and the whole group is joking and jesting, once more cheerful . . .

In Hudson Bay Peter Freuchen experienced a rather special case of wife-swapping. He travelled with a couple who were on their way to another couple living far away. Each spring the two couples met and changed partners. They stayed together for a whole year each in their own settlement and the next year they changed again.

But you do not visit a woman behind the back of her husband, warns Peter Freuchen. The man who dares go to a woman without having her husband's express permission, not only offends the husband grossly, but this breach of tradition and custom will give the man a bad reputation among his own people. His behaviour earns the contempt of everybody, and in many cases it requires immediate action by the husband. In order to save his honor he can pull his wife out of the hut and beat her in the presence of others.

151

Denmark had Her Heroes

"Perished in the 79-Fjord after trying to get home around the inland ice, in the month of November. I came here in a waning moon and could not get any further because of my frost-bitten feet and the dark. The bodies of the others can be found in the middle of the fjord in front of glacier (approx. 15 miles). Hagen died November 15th and Mylius 10 days later. Jörgen Brönlund."

This was the end of the Denmark-Expedition to the northeast coast of Greenland 1906-08. Denmark had her heroes.

Under the leadership of Mylius-Erichsen, the expedition was to explore and map the hitherto unexplored areas in Northeast Greenland. The expedition found a good anchoring place west of Cape Bismarck, the present Danmarkshavn, and here the 28 men, 90 dogs and an automobile wintered, until the sled voyages could begin in the spring. On March 28th two teams started. Mylius-Erichsen, Höegh-Hagen and Jörgen Brönlund made up one team, J. P. Koch, Tobias Gabrielsen and Aage Bertelsen the other.

On May 27th the two teams met each other rather unexpectedly at Cape Rigsdagen. At first they arranged to drive back to the ship together, as their tasks were done, but the next day Mylius-Erichsen had changed his mind. He wanted to continue west for a couple of days. On May 28th Mylius-Erichsen, Hagen and Brönlund drove west into Independence Sound, while Koch continued east. Weak from exhaustion his team reached the ship after a walk in the summer slush of snow and water which was several feet deep.

When Mylius-Erichsen's team had not returned in September, six search parties were dispatched from the ship. The last party returned on the 18th of October. No sign of the missing. They decided to wait until the light returned and on March 10th Koch and the Greenlander Tobias started a search. On March 19th they found Brönlund. He was lying in a rock cave. In a bottle they discovered his diary, written in the Greenland language. The message about the death of the others was written in Danish. Koch gave up the search for the bodies of the other two. A considerable amount of snow had fallen and Brönlund's reference to the location was too uncertain, Koch thought. Brönlund's feet were wrapped in rags, apparently his kamiks had been worn out and he had no sewing needle to repair them with.

All Denmark followed the expedition with good wishes. Even the matchboxes wished them a "Happy Journey!"

Mylius-Erichsen was a rather modern explorer for his time. He even brought an automobile. The photograph at right is of the landing in Danmarkshavn on June 17th, 1907

Mylius-Erichsen

Jörgen Brönlund   Höegh-Hagen   153

In the End they Ate Sand-Hoppers

The drama in East Greenland and Brönlund's diary attracted attention all over the world. Had Koch really looked enough for the bodies of the two others? Where were their diaries?

One day in 1909 a young and fearless Danish explorer, Ejnar Mikkelsen, was called to the office of Lord Northcliffe, the British newspaper magnate, who owned "The Daily Mail". Those diaries were to be found–with exclusive rights for "The Daily Mail", of course. "I'll pay the cost of the expedition. You just have to give the orders–and do your best," the newspaper Lord said.

Danish diaries going to a British newspaper? This was not Ejnar Mikkelsen's cup of tea. He quickly mobilized the committee of the Denmark Expedition. In Stavanger he found a 45-ton sloop, the ALABAMA, and following the traditional royal farewell wishes in Copenhagen–and a rather difficult voyage–he finally reached the coast of Eastern Greenland a couple of hundred miles south of the spot where the search was to begin. It was impossible to go further north because of the ice.

After a sled voyage of nine days they found the body of Brönlund. The fox

ALABAMA's winter camp at Shannon Island

The sad end of ALABAMA

The hut was made from the wreckage with the nameboard over the entrance

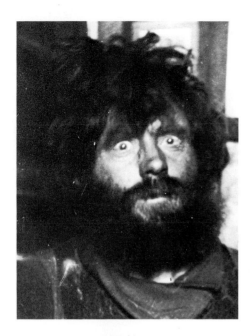

Ejnar Mikkelsen, the "savage" from the east coast, after the rescue. It is easy to understand why the Norwegian sealers were frightened

It had not been planned that Iver P. Iversen should participate in the tough expedition. He had been borrowed from another ship to repair the engine on the ALABAMA, but Ejnar Mikkelsen persuaded him to join them. At one point, when things were looking real bad, Iversen had hallucinations.
The chief engineer never joined another expedition. He had had enough

tracks showed them the way to the cave. They buried him properly under a cairn, but did not find the bodies of the others.

Brönlund's last words have been studied again and again, but no one has come any closer to the solution of the mystery. Recently the former head of the Greenland Department, Eske Brun, advanced a new theory. He does not believe that a Greenlander would use the Danish expression "omkom" (perished) and he feels it should be interpreted as "kom om", so that the message would read "Came around the 79-Fjord". Had Ejnar Mikkelsen known this theory at the time of the search, the result might have been different.

The people from the ALABAMA wintered on board the ship. And in April Ejnar Mikkelsen and his chief engineer, Iver P. Iversen, started on the 950 mile long sled voyage which was to take them to the places where there was a possibility of finding some of the cairns erected by the Denmark Expedition. It was to be a voyage which nearly cost them their lives. In a cairn in Danmark Fjord they found a cartridge with a message from Mylius-Erichsen. From this it appeared that they had killed seven dogs to feed themselves and the remaining dogs, while they lay for 16 days on the sea ice half a mile from the shore. They had been stopped by the melt water. The message ended on the confident note that they expected to reach the ship safely in 5-6 weeks.

Still further north the two men found a cairn with an account from which it was evident that the Peary Canal did not exist. After this the two Danes could do nothing but think of their own safety. They still had 625 miles back to the ship.

On June 1st they started east. Ejnar Mikkelsen had an attack of scurvy and in the end he could not even walk. He was tied to the sled. They found one of the caches laid out by the Denmark Expedition to cover Mylius-Erichsen's retreat. And they were very surprised because it could hardly be called a cache. It barely contained enough food for two men for a couple of days, even though the spot was marked on the map of the expedition as a cache.

They were still weak with hunger, but at least they had one comfort: Mikkelsen was cured of his scurvy after having eaten 13 raw sea gulls which Iversen had shot. Finally they were so ravenous that they ate sand-hoppers. In one whole day the two men caught only half a mugfull, and they tasted horrible. After a few days without food they had to eat the remaining two dogs, and just when everything seemed to be over, they found a new cache. But it contained only one box of provisions. The rest had been thrown to the dogs by the Denmark Expedition, as could be seen by the many split cans and all the excrements.

The two Danes were still alive when fall set in. They had to leave the sled and their sleeping bags and, in the end, their diaries, too. The men began to suffer from hallucinations, but in some miraculous way they suceeded in stumbling the final 50 miles to a small run-down hut in Danmarkshavn where they found food. Here, they stayed for a month and then continued the last 150 miles down to the ALABAMA. However, the ship had been wrecked. The crew had built a hut from the wreck and had left by another ship.

During the following winter Mikkelsen and Iversen walked the 450 miles back for the diaries which they had left on the way. Later in the summer, a small Norwegian sealer turned up near the hut. The two men looked so terrifying that the Norwegians were afraid to go up to them.

But they were saved–at last.

A 24,000-Mile Journey

When Knud Rasmussen and Peter Freuchen in Thule heard of the anxiety about the fate of Ejnar Mikkelsen and Iversen, they decided to start a rescue expedition across the 625 miles of the inland ice to Danmarks Havn. This was to be the 1st Thule Expedition and the beginning of Knud Rasmussen's fantastic career as one of the greatest arctic explorers of the world. His life was one long sled journey. It began in Jakobshavn, where he was the son of a pastor (he had very thin Greenland blood in his veins). Here Knud Rasmussen easily acquired what other arctic explorers had to learn at an adult age: the language, the handling of dogs, sled driving and the ability to survive even the worst hardships.

The two Danes did not find Mikkelsen, because he had taken a different route, and Mylius-Erichsen's cairn was empty.

The 2nd Thule Expedition had the purpose of mapping the last unknown part of Northern Greenland all the way to the northern tip. Among the participants was Dr. Lauge Koch, who was to chart the area, the Swedish botanist Dr. Thorild Wulff and from Thule, Peary's Harrigan and the interpreter Hendrik Olsen who had been a member of so many other expeditions.

The expedition took a very dramatic course. The hunting failed. 70 dogs were reduced to 18. It was then decided to split the expedition into two parties. Knud Rasmussen was to continue with the sleds to an agreed meeting place, while Wulfff, Lauge Koch, Hendrik Olsen and one other Greenlander were to walk overland along a stream.

To Knud Rasmussen's great surprise, Hendrik Olsen refused, but in the end he joined the others. Whatever happened after that has never been cleared up. Hendrik disappeared without a trace on a hunting trip to get some

provisions. They searched for him for twelve hours, but in vain. Had he been murdered by his hunting companion?

Wulff, too, lost his life. In the end he was too exhausted to walk and he asked the others to continue. If they had to carry him, they would all perish, he said. Just before he laid down to die, he wrote to Knud Rasmussen: "The constant lack of food and the hardships of the summer have reduced my strength to such an extent that I am no longer –even when summoning all my strength of will–able to follow Koch and the Eskimos. Since their rescue depends on getting to better hunting grounds as quickly as possible, it will only weigh

The Swedish botanist Dr. Thorild Wulff who never returned

heavily on them if I have to try to drag myself further. With peace of mind, I therefore say goodbye and thank you for good companionship during the expedition. I hope you will be able to save yourselves and our results."

When the others continued, Wulff had been waving and smiling to them.

Knud Rasmussen's 5th Thule Expedition, very humbly called "the long sled journey", became the most famous of

Harald Moltke's painting of Knud Rasmussen surrounded by his dogs

all. 24,000 miles from Greenland to the Pacific Ocean through the same regions where 75 years before the Franklin Expedition had perished.

This 5th Thule Expedition, which lasted from 1921 to 1924, brought home an enormous collection–a total of 15,000 items–which is now housed in the National Museum in Copenhagen.

On one sled journey which lasted a year and a half, Knud Rasmussen was only accompanied by two people from Thule–a widow, Arnarulunguak (meaning the little woman), and Mitek, the eider. They visited all the Eskimo tribes along the Pacific coast.

Knud Rasmussen was the last arctic explorer who fully employed the tradi-

tional Eskimo method of travelling. After him and also during his last expedition to Eastern Greenland modern techniques prevailed. The primitive life which had characterized arctic explorations for centuries was now replaced by airplanes, helicopters and snowmobiles. Slowly, modern technique was making its entry into Greenland.

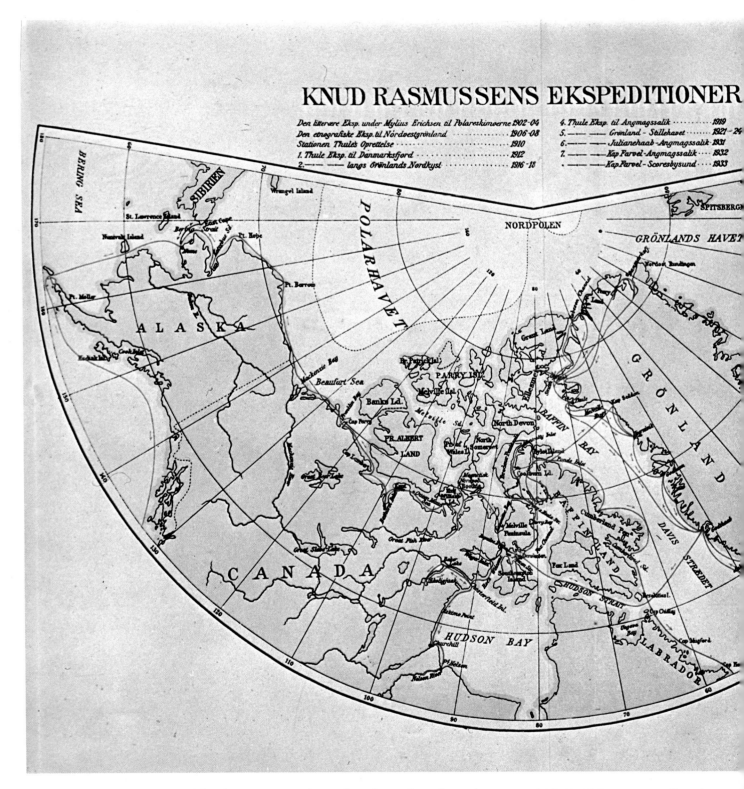

KNUD RASMUSSENS EKSPEDITIONER

Den litterære Eksp. under Mylius Erichsen til Polareskimoerne 1902-04
Den etnografiske Eksp. til Nordvestgrønland 1906-08
Stationen Thules Oprettelse 1910
1. Thule Eksp. til Danmarksfjord 1912
2. ———— langs Grønlands Nordkyst 1916-18

4. Thule Eksp. til Angmagssalik 1919
5. ———— Grønland – Stillehavet 1921-24
6. ———— Julianehaab –Angmagssalik· 1931
7. ———— Kap Farvel-Angmagssalik ··· 1932
·. ———— Kap Farvel – Scoresbysund ··· 1933

Knud Rasmussen's Expeditions. The above section of the northern hemisphere shows the routes which Knud Rasmussen followed on the long sled journeys which became his whole life. The longest of the journeys, the famous 5th Thule Expedition, from Greenland to the Pacific Ocean, covered no less than 24,000 miles

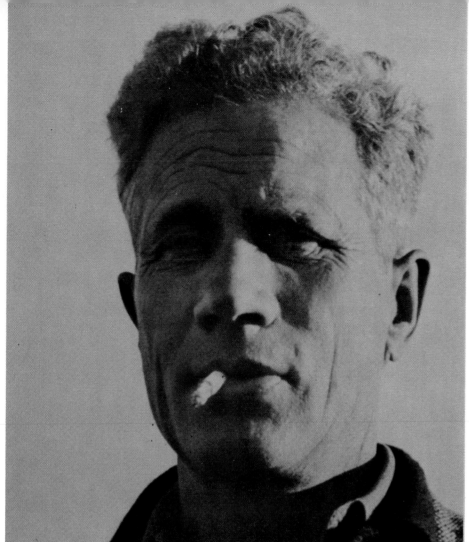

The last of the pioneers

The last in the long row of Danish pioneers, who have explored Greenland, is Eigil Knuth, known for his many Pearyland expeditions and year-long winterings. His excavations of Eskimo settlements in the northernmost part of Greenland have supported the theory that the earliest people in Greenland travelled north of Greenland and down along the east coast.

Credit is also due to Eigil Knuth for having "discovered" the exceptional Greenland artist Aron from Kangeq.

Knud Rasmussen with the beautiful Navarana in Angmagssalik 1933–the year when his remarkable life ended

On Horseback across the Inland Ice

Knud Rasmussen used the dog sled, J. P. Koch, a captain in the infantry, used something rather untraditional– horses. He had with him 16 Icelandic ponies when, in 1912, he took 40,000 pounds of equipment, provisions and food for the horses to the edge of the inland ice in Eastern Greenland. A weather station was to be established on the ice cap and the entire expedition had to winter. The three other members were the German geophysicist, Dr. Alfred Wegener, the Danish shipmaster Lars Larsen and the Icelander Vigfus Sigurdsson.

Following the wintering, the expedition started with five horses which were to take them across the inland ice at the widest point. At every rest-point they built a stable in the ice. Unfortunately, they had to shoot the ponies one by one, except one which was called Grauni. He kept going, but in the end he was so weak from exhaustion that the

men had to pull him on the sled. N. P. Koch wrote: "When he gave up this Morning, we bound his Legs, placed him on a Horse Blanket on Top of the Sleeping Bags between the two Sled Posts, covered him with two Reindeer skins and the Tent and tied him gently, but carefully to the Sled. There he lay with his Feed Bag, munching a Handfull of Concentrate and, seemingly, he enjoyed very much to be driven."

But Grauni did not make it. One hour's walk from a lovely West Greenland meadow he laid down and refused to eat. They left him, not having the heart to shoot him, and explored the coast.

Then they walked the long way back to the pony in the hope that he would be able to walk again, but he had to be shot.

At last they had only one dog, "Kamikdyret" (meaning the kamik critter) left as they sat on the island of

J. P. Koch in Danmarkshavn

Kangek, south of Upernavik, waiting for someone to spot them. They were crazy with hunger. Just as they were eating the dog raw, they saw a sail out in the fjord. They jumped down from the rocks, still munching the rest of the dog, and were saved by the pastor from Upernavik who was on his way to a confirmation in his umiak.

In 1930 Koch's companion, Dr.

On the way across the inland ice with "Grauni" and "Kamikdyret"

"Grauni" in his stable on the inland ice. When he was thirsty he just took a bite off the "crib"

Alfred Wegener

Alfred Wegener died in temperatures of 58° F. below, on a trip from the middle of the inland ice where his famous weather station "Eismitte" stood. The following year somebody found a pair of skies sticking out of the ice. Wegener's body lay two feet under the surface. All his travel equipment was untouched, only his diary was missing. Probably his companion, the 22-year old Greenlander Rasmus Villumsen had taken it and attempted to reach Umanak. He had perished too, but where? Villumsen was never found, even though a 2000 mile long search was made. Alfred Wegener was 50 years old. His name is specially linked with the theory about the continental shift.

Vigfus Sigurdsson on »Polaris«

Colonial Life Anno 1880

Approximately 300 people lived in Godthaab, the capital of Greenland, at the end of the previous century. Only five families were Danish, and they lived in style. They addressed each other in the third person and they never forgot their titles. These were the people whom Mylius-Erichsen, in his attack on the governing body in Greenland, described as the narrow-minded provincials from the pocket state of Denmark.

The previous dean in Greenland, G. N. Bugge, who was the son of a colony manager from Godthaab, has told about life in the Greenland of those days in lectures and later in articles in the magazine "Greenland". Bugge grew up in Hans Egede's house which was built of big boulders. The people lived primarily from the country's own products. Two pounds of reindeer meat cost 10-12 öre. On the other hand, the people did not make much money. When the ships arrived the local people were hired to help with the unloading. The daily wage for a Greenlander, working from six in the morning until six in the evening, was 1 Danish krone.

Godthaab had Greenland's first hospital. According to Dr. Bertelsen the inventory included: 2 beadsteads, 1 mattress, 9 blankets, 2 air rings, 1 wooden table, 1 cupboard, 2 bathtubs, 4 spitting mugs, 1 bedpan, 3 iron pans, 4 wooden splints and a fracture apparatus. The spitting mugs could be found only on the inventory. Beds were non-existent, the patients lay on planks.

A new hospital was being built, however, and in 1907 the town's sanitary conditions were considerably improved, especially when it was ordered that the cuspidors from the church must not be emptied into the streams from which the Greenlanders fetched their drinking water.

Aside from Christmas, the biggest annual celebration was the king's birthday. The officials were loyal and so was the population, even though they had never seen their king. The closest they came to having seen royalty was Prins Valdemar, who had been on board the naval ship FYLLA during its tour of inspection in 1886. But he was also received in style. The colony manager in Frederikshaab sailed out to the ship in his kayak, with his black silk hat tied to his head. He was hoisted on board, kayak, silk hat and all, so that he could receive the prince with dignity.

Another royal function was also celebrated in the approved fashion. This was the 40th anniversary of king Christian IX's reign. Dean Bugge wrote that, "The directors in Copenhagen had given special instructions as to what should be done. In the morning all flags were run up, and at the same time the cannons on the flag station fired a salute. Apart from the usual extras, which the population received on festive occasions, such as grain, peas and hard bread, they had coffee, cigars and Christmas cake on this occasion. After the Danish sermon in the afternoon–the Greenland sermon was probably held in the morning–all Danes gathered for coffee in the pastor's house. Later, figs were thrown for the Greenland children from the second floor of the house. In the evening they watched fireworks, prepared and fired by the photographer John Möller. Then the dancing began in the carpenter's workshop, which had been decorated for the occasion with a huge banner depicting the king's monogram and crown. The walls were decorated with flags and the windows had curtains made of coloured paper. Two violins and an accordion supplied the music. The Greenland women were dressed in all their fineries and everyone was in high spirits. The Danes, who had just come to watch, were soon affected by the happy atmosphere and took part in the dancing, completely forgetting their usual superiority.

Inside view of a Danish colony home during the eighties

That was how a great hunter lived–a very wealthy Greenlander

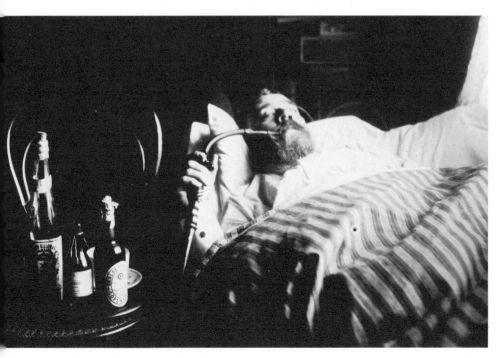

Life in the colonies did not lack style. When Mr. Möller in Ivigtut was ill,
Dr. Bertelsen took this picture of him

Two Danish officials in a tent.
Apparently they were not short of anything 165

The Rich Danes -

The colony manager and his wife. The lady's fancy hat was not exactly the proper thing for the Greenland climate

Class distinction existed among the Danes, too. The settlement traders belonged to the lower class. They handled the trade in the smaller settlements and they often married Greenland women

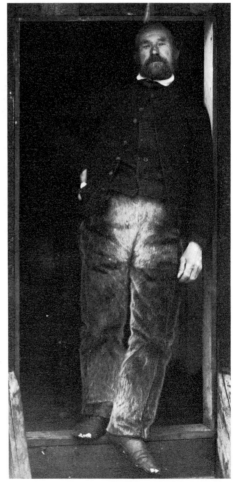

Danish colonial types. They had an arrogant air about them. They were used to giving orders and did not expect anybody to contradict them

and the Impoverished Greenlanders

A Greenland winter home

Isaias from Julianehaab

The hunter's dance is the name of these steps. Probably it was a Scottish reel which the Greenlanders learned during the whaling times. The picture is taken in Godthaab in 1872 and the occasion must be particularly festive, possibly the king's birthday, for at right somebody is serving aquavit and this happened only on festive occasions

Joel and his wife Kornelia

Agto in Northern Greenland

Greenland woman washing clothes

A Busy Geologist

In 1876 the young Andreas Kornerup came to Greenland, working as a geologist and assistant on several expeditions to the Julianehaab district. He was very industrious, as if he had a premonition that his life was going to be very short and, therefore, he had to be very busy. He was only 24 years old when he died from pulmonary tuberculosis.

Kornerup graduated in applied science when only 21 years old and became a lecture in soil science at the Royal Veterinary and Agricultural College in Copenhagen. Even though very young, he was known as a brilliant scientist, but he was also an artist and a painter. The pictures here, which Kornerup painted during his last stay in Greenland in 1879–the year before he died– have never before been published. They are now kept at the Trade and Maritime Museum at Kronborg Castle in Elsinore.

An umiak at Isortoq

The colony at Holsteinsborg

Greenland peat hut

169

Greenland's first Color Photographer

Pastor P. Rüttel, who came to Angmagssalik in 1894 as the first missionary in Eastern Greenland, understood his own historical importance, just like Hans Egede had before him. However, Rüttel was a much more modern missionary. Instead of a sketchbook he brought a camera, and over the years he took thousands of photographs on glass plates.

Just after the turn of the century Rüttel was back in Denmark on leave and then he journeyed back, this time to Southern Greenland. During the stay in Denmark he had taught himself a new, but extremely difficult photographic technique. By pouring several layers of emulsion over the glass plates, he was able to expose the pictures in color. He thus became Greenland's first color photographer.

When, in the summer of 1971, Major J. Helk, the director of the Arctic Institute in Copenhagen, went through Rüttel's huge collection of pictures, which is kept at the institute, he was rather startled. He found color on one of the glass plates. It turned out that the collection included several color photos. Some of them are published here for the very first time.

It has been impossible to date these photographs with certainty, but they were probably taken during the first decade of this century.

A young Greenlander who is probably better educated than most of his compatriots. His fancy scarf is rather untypical of a Greenlander

Spring in Nanortalik

Peat huts near Godthaab. In the background Hjortetak Mountain

Two young girls—possibly Danish—clad in Greenland dress

Two Danish children playing with a doll. It is not known who they are

Below. Mrs. Helga Rüttel

Pastor Rüttel also took pictures of himself

The Councilor Reform

Up to the middle of the 19th century, no major changes took place in the small colonies managed by the Danes. However, Dr. H. J. Rink, the inspector for Southern Greenland–who in many ways meant more to the Greenlanders than Hans Egede did–realized that the Greenlanders had to have greater influence on their own affairs. At his suggestion the so-called councils were established at the beginning of the 1860's. They were a sort of local governments which, for the first time, gave the Greenlanders a voice in their own affairs. It was not much, but it was a beginning, anyhow.

A council was established for each colony district, consisting of ex-officio members, the Danish clergymen, doctors, colony managers and assistants, and of chosen Greenlanders, councilors (with red caps), who were the population's representatives with the authorities. Furthermore, they had a certain authority in their respective settlements.

The councils met twice a year to discuss various Greenland problems, for instance aid in the form of prizes or encouragement, relief for the poor and, according to certain set rules, the distribution of the state revenue, a sort of return to the hunters and the supporters. The councils also settled smaller disputes between the Greenlanders, held inquiries when a crime was committed and made recommendations to the inspector regarding the punishment.

The system had one serious flaw–the inspector had to attend to the economic interests of the trade company and, at the same time, to the material and spiritual needs of the Greenlanders.

H. J. Rink understood this quite clearly, and as the best solution, he suggested a clearer separation of trade and administration. Later, when he was director of the Royal Greenland Trade Company, he established a committee, functioning as an intermediate link between the Department of the Interior

Rink introduced the councils. As a sign of their office the councilors wore red caps with cockades which gave them a certain military look. But there was absolutely nothing soldierly about them!

and the inspectors. Rink had strong opponents in the department, however, and after several years of dispute he resigned his directorship and left Denmark a disappointed man. He died in Oslo in 1893. His successor was Hugo E. Hörring, his most ardent opponent.

After Rink's resignation excitement about conditions in Greenland subsided, but then Mylius-Erichsen spoke up. Following his expedition in 1904 he sharpened his pen, and it was very pointed indeed. He attacked the Danish administrative system and the whole matter became a mighty controversy, the issue of which was a new law about the management of Greenland.

Mylius-Erichsen was clearly influenced by two Danish rebels in Greenland, C. W. Schulz-Lorenzen, pastor and principal of the seminary, and Gustav Koppel, the doctor in Godthaab. These

According to the Rink reform the Greenlanders had some sort of contributory influence. Among other things, they had to sign the minutes of the meetings

H. J. Rink was a man of many talents. During his travels in Greenland he always carried his sketchbook with him. Here is his impression of Godhavn, established in 1782 and until 1950 the main seat of the inspectors in Northern Greenland

two men had the most furious disagreement about the Greenland policy, with the trade company's representative, even though they played tarot in the evenings. Finally, the authorities excluded Schulz-Lorenzen from participation in the council meetings, despite his being an ex-officio member.

Mylius-Erichsen's attack almost developed into a criminal accusation against the director of the trade company, who had to clear himself through a trial at which he was acquitted.

But the mistaken Greenland policy was not acquitted, and thanks to a new and more progressive parliament a proposal, worked out by the inspector in Godhavn, was accepted. He suggested for one thing, that the officials left the local councils, which were then made into town councils, and secondly, he recommended that two provincial coun-

cils should be established, one for Northern and one for Southern Greenland. The law of 1908 separated trade and administration, but as this brought about total chaos, the entire management was combined under one director, with a chief of trade in Greenland as his advisor. The proposer himself became the director, and for a generation he was the autocratic, if gentle ruler of Greenland.

The time up to World War II was only marked by small general changes, even though one big reform was introduced, on paper at least. This was the law of 1925. For the first time nothing was said about Greenland being self-supporting. The law had as its aim that the Greenlanders should be educated so that they would be able to have free relations with the rest of the world, when the isolation would be ended.

173

The Bears in East Greenland Are also Danes

During the interwar period, life in Greenland went its quiet colonial way, interrupted only by a single arctic storm that swept over Eastern Greenland. It was raised by some Norwegian hunters and by a Norwegian flag in no man's land, otherwise only occupied by seals and polar bears.

Actually, Denmark and Norway had made a pact in 1924 about the Norwegians' right to hunt in the uninhabited areas of Eastern and Northeastern Greenland. But Norway still claimed that the regions were no man's land, while Denmark maintained that all of Greenland was Danish. It did not matter much about the flags, but when the Norwegian government provided certain hunters with police authority–and thus officially acknowledged the occupation, the Danes were alarmed.

The dispute grew more and more bitter with attacks and counterattacks in the Danish and Norwegian press. Even Knud Rasmussen, who was usually very objective, let himself be carried away. In a lecture on the exploration of Greenland he quite "forgot" the Norwegian explorers, such as Nansen, Sverdrup, Amundsen and Astrup, whereas he stressed the Swedish expeditions in Greenland.

In the end, Denmark appealed to the International Court at the Hague, and here–in 1933–the court sustained Denmark's claim: All of Greenland is Danish. Two judges voted against the decision.

Afterwards Denmark and Norway could demonstrate to the rest of the world that this is a dignified way for two nations to settle a mutual dispute.

174   *There are still hunting cabins in Eastern Greenland. This very exclusive cabin is standing on Sandodden*

Teufelschloss in Kejser Franz Joseph Fjord is one of the regions of beautiful scenery which the Hague decision awarded to Denmark

This polar bear has a court decision about his Danish citizenship

Hunting cabin from the Norwegian times. It is primitive, but a man could live here alone for 2½ years–without going mad

175

Hands Off Greenland

Greenland was nearly occupied by Canada right after the German occupation of Denmark on April 9th 1940. It was the valuable cryolite that attracted, plus the fear that the Germans might establish long-range air bases in Eastern Greenland. The Canadian occupation had been arranged with Great Britain, but the United States asked the Canadians to keep their hands off Greenland.

The Americans referred to the Monroe Doctrine of 1820, according to which the status quo is to be preserved in the European areas of the Western hemisphere.

Greenland escaped becoming part of Canada, but it did not become American either, even though, in 1941 Henrik Kauffmann, who was the Danish ambassador in Washington, D.C., signed "The agreement relating to the defence of Greenland". This agreement gave the Americans the right to establish bases in specific uninhabited areas and the right to patrol Greenland waters. In return for supplies of cryolite for the production of aluminum, Canada and the United States committed themselves to keeping Greenland supplied with provisions as long as the war lasted and

it was cut off from the motherland.

The Greenland agreement had the effect that the German-controlled Danish government was forced to remove Henrik Kauffmann from his post, whereupon he continued as if nothing had happened.

The chief administrative officer in Southern Greenland, Eske Brun, did the same. He handled the administration and the "army" which consisted of a handful of ex-hunters, now united in "The North-East Greenland Sledge Patrol"–or as they were called the Sledge Patrol.

They drive tens of thousands of miles. A trivial, lonely job which has but one purpose: to prevent a repetition of the Hague case

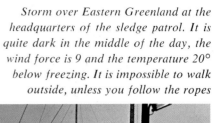

Ready for camping in the wilderness

Storm over Eastern Greenland at the headquarters of the sledge patrol. It is quite dark in the middle of the day, the wind force is 9 and the temperature 20° below freezing. It is impossible to walk outside, unless you follow the ropes

The weather in Greenland determines the weather in Europe, and, therefore, weather forecasts for Greenland were of military importance for the air raids on both Great Britain and Germany. It was anticipated that the Germans would establish weather stations on the desolate eastern coast of Greenland, and this was the reason for establishing the sledge patrol. All through the war the patrol warred more against cold and loneliness than it did against the Germans.

The members of the patrol, which consisted primarily of Danes, a few Norwegians and a good many Greenlanders, were provided with police authority from the governing body in Godthaab. In pairs they drove tens of thousands of miles across the wilds of Eastern Greenland to keep an eye on the Germans.

And the Germans did come. They established several weather stations which the patrol reported to the Americans. One of the stations which had 27 men was attacked by six men from the sledge patrol. However, the attack was discovered too early by the military leader of the station. He ran right into one member of the patrol, when going grouse hunting with his fowling piece.

The Dane ordered him to lay down his gun which he did, but he also pulled out his pistol with his left hand and succeeded in firing one shot before he was shot down with a machine gun. The Danish attack had been revealed but the result was nevertheless that the Germans very quickly left the weather station. Their trawler, which was moored in the ice, was blown up and the crew picked up by airplanes.

There were other skirmishes with the Germans. Once the leader of the sledge patrol, captain Ib Poulsen, was attacked in a cabin at Sabine Island, but he escaped under cover of the darkness —without dogs and sleds. He walked 80 miles to Eskimonaes where the patrol had their station. Here they prepared themselves for a German attack. The Germans arrived when it got dark and asked if the Danes were going to shoot. The answer was yes, even though they were only three men with old fashioned pistols and rifles against the Germans' automatic weapons. The Danes escaped from the cabin, however, without a scratch and walked more than 200 miles south, on foot and without equipment, in the biting winter cold.

Three others of the patrol ran into a German ambush. Corporal Eli Knud-

The sledge patrol cooperated with the American forces. When they had located a German weather station, the Americans were notified. The picture is taken during an American attack on a German weather station

sen was shot as he tried to escape. Shortly after, two others, Marius Jensen and Peter Nielsen ran into the same ambush and were captured. They were taken to Germaniahavn. Peter Nielsen got the Germans' permission to go down and bury Eli Knudsen, but beforehand he had arranged with Marius Jensen that he would simply run off and join the rest of the patrol on Ella Island.

Marius Jensen now became driver for the German commander, a lieutenant Ritter. During a tour of inspection Marius Jensen, who was about to feed the dogs, discovered that the German had left his rifle on the sled. This changed the balance of power and now it was Ritter who was the prisoner. It took Marius Jensen and the German 19 days to travel 300 miles down to Scoresby Sound. At night he locked the prisoner inside a hunting cabin or he

let him sleep in a tent, while he himself slept on the sled so far away that the German would not be able to reach him. Ritter knew very well that if he ran off in this unknown region he would be lost. Furthermore, Marius Jensen let him walk in front of the sled every day, and in the evening he was too tired to think of escaping. Lieutenant Ritter walked about freely in Scoresby Sound, until he was picked up by an American plane.

When the war was over the sledge patrol continued to patrol the desolate regions in Eastern Greenland, but the name was changed to "Siriuspatruljen" (the Sirius patrol). As the picture on the opposite page indicates, more modern transport equipment has now been put into service. Eastern Greenland is no longer a no man's land which anybody can claim.

This was all that was left. The Germans had disappeared and the weather station was burned down.

Once a year, in June, the entire patrol meets at Daneborg where everybody enjoys the fabolous Danish "cold table"– and they are even wearing a tie!

The Sirius patrol now gets its provisions by plane, dumping caches along the thousand mile long route which the men have to follow on their long tour of inspection. The picture is from Ella Island, the second largest of the patrol stations

Crash Landing on the Ice Cap

The Greenlanders were hardly aware of the American presence in Greenland during the war–aside from the fact that they were rather well-supplied with American products and once in a while saw an American on a short visit. For a while, there were actually more Americans than Greenlanders in Greenland, but they were stationed in desolate, isolated spot.

The agreement with the Danish governing body in Greenland made it possible for the Americans to establish air bases. And one fine summer day, American bulldozers rolled onto the Greenland coast and cut their way into the first landing strip. The base was located at Narssarssuaq, in convenient proximity to the essential cryolite. Then came the second base, Bluie West Eight, near Söndre Strömfjord and finally a third base in Eastern Greenland not too far from Angmagssalik. Apart from these air bases a series of weather stations were established.

The bases were used as intermediate landing grounds for the fighters and bombers going from the American assembly lines to the British air bases. A gigantic, but troublesome air lift of planes flying across the inland ice was established, sometimes causing many mishaps and accidents. Many planes had to force-land on the inland ice and survival techniques were not as advanced as they are to-day.

The biggest emergency landing took place one day in July in the middle of the war. Six planes, two Flying Fortresses and four fighters, had to force-land on the ice at one time. They had

Brigadier General in the U.S. Air Force, Bernt Balchen, who organized the construction of the American air bases in Greenland during World War II. Balchen, who was born in Norway 1899, was pilot for Admiral Byrd on his Antarctic expedition 1928-30. Balchen has described his experiences in Greenland in the book, "War below Zero".

This photograph of one of the crashed pilots shows how the Americans managed. Sheltered by the wing flaps of the Flying Fortresses they pitched a tent and set up a primitive stove so they could make some hot chocolate

flown into heavy fog and their heaters and air-pressure gauges froze. When the planes got into trouble above the inland ice, the pilot, in code, requested a weather forecast from the Bluie West base in Southern Greenland. The coded answer told them that the base was closed because of thick fog and they were to try to land on Bluie West Eight, further north.

The planes changed course and flew right into even worse weather. They sent off another request and once more the answer was: Continue north. Finally, they had to go down. All of the 25 men in the six planes escaped practically unharmed from this, the biggest collective emergency landing in Greenland.

When they were finally rescued from the ice, they had the surprise of their lives. They could perfectly well have landed on Bluie West One, where the weather had been fine.

Without firing a single shot the Germans had put six planes out of action forever. The famous Norwegian-American flyer, Major Bernt Balchen who had been responsible for the establishing of the American bases in Greenland, disclosed that a German u-boat or a secret station on the east coast had deciphered the American code and directed the planes to a spot where the weather was worse.

After the war the base in Southern Greenland was shut down. To-day it is the headquarters for the Danish ice reconnaissance patrol.

The other base, Bluie West Eight, is still used, and when an American tourist makes a stop here on his way to a vacation in Europe, he invariably asks, "Are we back in the U.S.?"

You cannot blame the tourists for asking, because apart from the Greenland souvenir shop in the lobby of the hotel and the Danish flag, Söndre Strömfjord is a "little America".

One of the Flying Fortresses in the air

When Bluie West One had localized the stranded planes provisions were dropped to the 25 men on the ice

Danes, but only on Paper

They became Danes on paper. Their essential European background was pinned on the wall

After the war, the Danish prime minister, Hans Hedtoft, taught the Greenlanders to sing the nursery rhyme about little Peter Spider, but he did much more than that. During meetings, in 1948, with the two chief administrative officers, he informed them that this was the beginning of a new era and that Greenland had to come out of its isolation. That same year a great Greenland Commission was established, and two years later it gave its opinion leading to an amendment of the Danish constitution in 1953.

At that time, Greenland–at the express wish of the Greenlanders–became a part of Denmark on an equal footing with the rest of the country.

At the beginning, the United Nations had difficulty in accepting this. It was unthinkable that a colony could become independent in any other way than by breaking away from the motherland. If the United Nations accepted Denmark's action, more imperialist states might be tempted to call their colonies "a part of the country with equal rights". However, the two newly elected members of parliament from Greenland convinced the General Assembly at the United Nations that it was the Greenlanders' desire to become Danes on equal footing with all other Danish citizens.

Greenland became Danish and the Greenlanders became Danes, but only on paper. Only about 20 percent of the population speak Danish to-day, even though every other living Greenlander is born in the free Greenland and not in the colony.

It is still so–so with Greenland independence, but this has an explanation. Greenland plays the role of the receiver and, therefore, it is to a large extent dependent on the giver. The Danish development assistance to Greenland amounts to approx. 100 million dollars

a year. How much of that goes back into Danish pockets is quite a different matter.

The greatest stumbling-block in Danish-Greenland relations it the so-called birthplace criterion, which means that Greenlanders employed by the state have a lower salary than their Danish colleagues in Greenland. This criterion has given rise to numerous protests, even though the provincial council voted unanimously on it. The birthplace criterion was based on the fact that Greenland was an economic unity with a price

policy very different from Denmark's, and that the salaries should be raised concurrently with the bearing capacity of the individual occupations. But principle is one thing, feeling is another. The Greenlanders find the birthplace criterion discriminatory, even though the country is probably one of the few areas in the world where race discrimination has never truly existed.

In any case, the elevation from being a colony meant that something began to happen in the development of Greenland.

The plank bed is something characteristic of Greenland. Neither the amendment to the constitution nor modern Danish architecture have been able to get rid of it

Ten years after the equality of status with the rest of the country you could still see buildings like these. In this shack a mother lived with her nine children

The New Land

The great Commission had been in labour and had given birth to a building site. The following years, thousands of Danish workmen invaded the sleepy little towns in Western Greenland, and the dynamite parties woke them up with a start.

The gnarled rocks had to give way to hospitals, schools, homes, workshops, factories, power stations, roads. One of the problems which the great Commission had insisted on solving first was the battle against Greenland's national scourge, tuberculosis. The help came from an unexpected quarter.

Following a visit to Greenland, Queen Ingrid summoned the prime minister and some leading politicians to the royal palace. She expressed her alarm at what she had seen in Greenland and offered to make funds of her own available in an attempt to help build a sanatorium. A few weeks after this meeting, the first hospital barracks were on their way.

The first stage of the present Dronning Ingrid's Hospital in Godthaab is the fastest building operation which has been accomplished in Greenland. Developments were quick in other areas too. Some thought too quick. The Greenlanders could not keep the pace. They became spectators. Passive. It is easier to introduce electricity than it is to introduce a new form of life. An entire generation of uneduacted Greenlanders were about to be destroyed.

The only medicine seemed to be education and retraining. This has been started in all areas. Together with the new towns, a generation of better equipped Greenlanders is growing up. 100 million dollars worth of Danicization is being sent across the Atlantic Ocean every year, equivalent to well over 10,000 dollars annually per household. But even though the contours of the Greenland towns are being straightened out and the self-made houses are being replaced by surburban housing, designed by an architect, there will always be an unchangeable Greenland.

Greenland is still the land of the great contrasts, in nature as well as in way of life. Some of Greenland has become Danish, but most of it is still Greenland.

Greenland's biggest Building Site

Godthaab is the biggest building site in Greenland. The Commission had decided that the future lay in the towns which were navigable all year through: Frederikshaab, Godthaab, Sukkertoppen and Holsteinsborg.

Out of the first Danish-built hovels of no more than 350 sq. ft., containing only the plank bed from the earthen hut, entirely new housing types have emerged, and during recent years even modern building blocks have shot up.

Danish companies have become experts in arctic building construction. During the first years it was a long way from the drawing board in Copenhagen to the tough realities of Greenland. In Narssaq some of the first Danish-built houses flew away because no one, despite the Greenlanders' warnings, had taken into consideration the very special wind conditions in that area. In Holsteinsborg the new shop all of a sudden started to wriggle like a snake, because it had been forgotten that even permafrost may start to thaw. And in Godthaab some buildings were erected with doors so narrow that not even an ordinary easy chair could be moved in. In the course of time, quite a few million Danish kroner have been blown across the Greenland mountains. But this is nothing compared to what has been achieved–good or bad.

Everything went fast. Not only were the omissions of the colonial times going to be alleviated, but everything had to be built in a race with the greatest population explosion in history. The statisticians anticipated that Godthaab with its present 7000 inhabitants would, within the foreseeable future, reach a figure of 25,000.

In the meantime a few problems have emerged. For one thing, the climate has changed for the worse, so that the basis of existence for the towns, the cod, may disappear. Secondly, the population may

The Greenland bedrock has to give way to to-day's modern pneumatic drills

Godthaab is probably one of the most beautiful building sites in the world. New housing blocks are shooting up with record speed. But will it be possible, in the future, to find work for all these people who are going to live here?

not experience the explosion the planners had figured on. Admittedly, it was impossible to make the Greenlanders buy "The little green with the bear" (a contraceptive with a polar bear as a trade mark), sold from vending machines which almost never worked because of the cold. But the spiral forms part of family planning, and the surplus population has been rapidly reduced.

Furthermore, some people doubt whether it is right to concentrate the population in big towns without a particular basis of existence. The golden times, created by the provision of Danish capital, will be over some day. Godthaab is still Klondike and the Treasury the big goldmine, but like all other goldmines it might some day be empty.

Everything for the Customers

Assistance to Greenland is sent primarily in the form of provisions and equipment. Every year 200,000 tons of goods are sailed across the Atlantic Ocean to Greenland. This is done in huge arctic ships which berth directly at the quay in the places where they have one. At other places the cargo must be loaded into barges and sailed ashore.

The times are gone when the eggs were rotten, the ryebread mouldy and when people in the shop in Godthaab almost fought over a head of cabbage. The Royal Greenland Trade Company has the responsibility for supplies and the company takes this responsibility very seriously. Not only does it have to supply its own shops, but it also has to provide for their competitors.

Until 1960 provisions were rather short in some places. The construction of the harbors had not been finished and the loading into barges took time. At some places it was a matter of readjusting to modern times. A few years back a Danish scientist got the following answer when he wanted to buy an axe from the shopkeeper (an obstinate ex-colony manager). "I'll take your name down. You can come back next year. I'm not going to order any more axes this year."

But those times are gone too. To-day, private business people have taken over a large part of the trade and this has meant better service for the customers. Many of the new business people are former workmen who started on a small scale in a shack. Now, with good loan possibilities and the lack of taxes, many of them count their profits in the millions. Almost no shops with a reasonable turnover are owned by Greenlanders. The native population looks through the windows at the rich society.

Only very few places have a deep-water quay. If not, the loading is done the traditional way

Greenland's biggest supply ship, M/S MAYUMBE, *in Godthaab harbor*

The bakery in Godthaab might just as well be situated in Copenhagen. There's no difference. Even the shopgirl is Danish

She has been to the local Greenland shop, to get a Norwegian haddock for dinner. In each town there is a place near the harbor where the hunters and smaller fishermen sell the products they have brought home. The prices are determined by supply and demand—and ability to speak the language. The Danes have taken the hint—as a rule they send their Greenland domestic servant

In the cooperative supermarket. Girl with oranges. You can buy them all year round

189

It Was the World's Best Arctic Ship

It was the end of January, 1959, in Godthaab. The next day, the Greenland ship HANS HEDTOFT, the big new state passenger ship on her maiden voyage, was leaving for the towns in Southern Greenland and then for Denmark. The captain declared that he had the world's best arctic ship, and that he would set a new Atlantic record. Another captain warned him though: "There is a lot of snow around Cape Farewell, so go far south. Don't get to close." But the captain of HANS HEDTOFT maintained that he was going to beat all previous records. On January 30th at 1745 hours the ship hit an iceberg 27 nautical miles southeast of Cape Farewell in a blind-

The passengers going on board in Godthaab

Boat drill is a standing ritual when you sail to and from Greenland

ing snowstorm. The ship had a gaping leak into the engine room. The water was streaming in. The main engine and other machinery stopped. The ship was drifting around helplessly in the hurricane.

The first distress signal from the ship read, HAVE HIT ICEBERG. WATER IN ENGINE ROOM IS RISING. ASSISTANCE NECESSARY. The German trawler JOHANNES KRÜSS from Bremerhaven was out in the same hurricane and in the same area. The trawler was in radio contact with HANS HEDTOFT fifteen times, but just as the trawler was at the position which had been quoted by the sinking ship, they received the last signal: AM SINKING SLOWLY. URGENT ASSISTANCE NEEDED. Then came two drawn-out signals. The radio officer had sent out signals on his emergency sender, calmly and steadily until the water took him.

The German trawler continued the search among 30 feet high waves and almost hit an iceberg herself. At the same time the hitherto biggest international search near Greenland was initiated. Icelandic, American, Canadian and Danish rescue planes searched for days on end. Nothing was found. Much later a lifebuoy from HANS HEDTOFT drifted ashore on Iceland. This is the only thing ever found of the ship and its 95 passengers and crew members. Among them was the member of parliament from Greenland, Augo Lynge. Two years earlier he had warned Parliament of winter voyages with passengers, but his warning was brushed aside by Johannes Kjaerböll who was the Minister for Greenland.

After the loss of HANS HEDTOFT a new storm broke loose; this time in Den-

HANS HEDTOFT, *on her maiden voyage, leaving Godthaab harbor to meet her fate at Cape Farwell*

mark. It turned out that the captains sailing to Greenland had been pressed to make a statement about the winter sailings which was in direct contradiction to an earlier statement they had made. In the first statement they warned against winter voyages, in the other they supported them, which suited the minister perfectly, since this second statement he could use in Parliament as an argument for the building of the state ship.

The director of the Royal Greenland Trade Company disclosed that the minister had dismissed the first statement as useless. The minister declared that he had never seen or heard of the first statement. There was a conflict of evidence, and an examining judge from the Supreme Court was unable to ascertain who spoke the truth. Johannes Kjaerböl was nearly saddled with an impeachment–but was finally let off.

The big commission examined the circumstances of the shipwreck, but was never informed of the conversation between the two captains.

Since this loss, all passenger voyages to Greenland in the period December -March have been prohibited.

191

By Ship and by Sloop - by Sled and by Chopper

Each year the administration in Godthaab receives inquiries from abroad, especially from the United States and Great Britain, as for instance the following. "Please let me know the train times for the cities on the west coast of Greenland." Or, "Would you kindly send me a road map, since I plan to drive from South to North Greenland."

There is no road between the towns of Greenland other than the air, water- or ice road. But these are used frequently enough. Each year approx. 35,000 people sail by the modern passenger ships which run between the towns or by the small boat into the fjords.

The big coastal ship Kununguaq with 100 passengers, cafeteria and soft music outside Narssarssuaq

Where there is no deep-water quay, the passengers go ashore by motorboat

One of the small passenger boats on its way into Godthaab Fjord

One of Greenlandair's helicopters preparing to land. The equipment must be first-class in order to withstand the Greenland weather

And 25,000 fly annually by Greenlandair's Sikorsky helicopters. That is what the statistics say, anyway. But there is no mention of how many travel by dog sled. This means of transport is the only one available when the waters are closed by the ice.

Local flying in Greenland did not start until ten years ago, using old Catalinas and Canadian Sea Otters. To-day only helicopters are used.

The dog sled is on the wane as a means of transportation in Greenland. Up north, however, it is indispensable. At a spot on the horizon an obelisk has been erected in memory of Peary

A rich -

In some places Greenland has become an affluent society. To-day it is almost dangerous to walk in Skibshavnsvej in Godthaab, where traffic is very heavy even if you see the same cars many times when you walk along the road.

During the summer the Danish workmen work 16 hours a day in order to provide the setting for planned welfare, so that the Greenland woman, in her modern kitchen, is able to enjoy the national drink, coffee.

Even Greenland has its abandoned cars and soon they will have a junk yard, but the children are having fun.

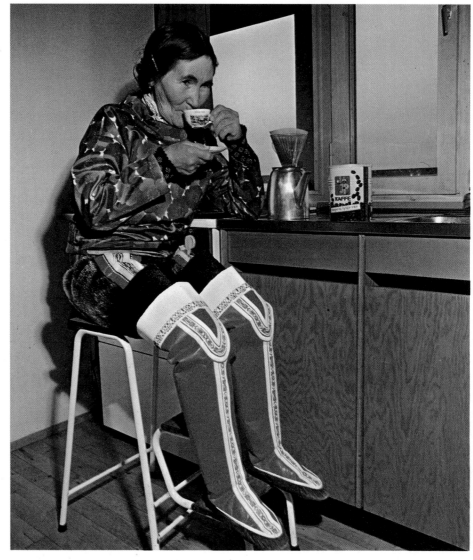

and a poor Country

It is not all welfare, however. The girl down at the harbor, who is collecting coke in a bag, so that the family can have a small fire in the stove, or the woman who has to go out and hack off a piece of ice with a pair of scissors to put in the water kettle–they do not belong to the affluent society. And it is difficult for a people of hunters to adjust to living in a housing block. After all, when you do not have any storage room what do you do then?

Some places in Godthaab they have lavatories. In Kangamiut they only have the Alter Room–but plenty of fresh air.

Tourist Country without Tourists

Even though Danish initiative is leaving deep scars on the towns of Western Greenland, the efforts to create an architecture which blends with the surroundings have succeeded many places. But it is painful while it lasts. At one time it was so bad that a pastor had to complain. He could hardly hear himself preach on Sundays for the endless blasting around town. And the pneumatic drills. But they are always noisy whether they are used for road construction or for digging a grave before a burial.

To-day, Greenland is a blend of old and new attractions for the tourists–but there are very few tourists. At the beginning of the sixties, charter travel started on a small scale, but the big mass invasion at low prices has not yet been seen in this obvious tourist land. This is in part due to the hotel shortage, in part to the waywardness of the arctic climate. You can never trust a 12-day tourist trip to last twelve days. When the arctic

weather gods go into action, they do it properly. Maybe that is why the word *imaqa* is the word most frequently used in the Greenland language. To-morrow –imaqa.

But if the tourist is willing to take a chance–and can afford to–there is plenty to see in this great land. In Southern

Julianehaab's most popular tourist motif: Greenland's only fountain

The arrival of a ship is always a big event and the harbor is swarming with children. Pleasures are few and, furthermore, half of the population is under 14

*The church in Jakobshavn with the
fjord in the background*

Greenland he may experience the balmy
idyl in the mediaeval towns or go fishing
in the fjords with every chance of
catching salmon. Further up north he
has views of the eternal ice and towns
which even Hans Egede would recognize.

All summer there are established
connections by coastal ships from Julianehaab in the south to Upernavik in
the north, but only on an individual
basis.

In a few years, however, the jumbo
jet-age will have reached Greenland,
too, and the tourist invasion will begin.

*Main street in Holsteinsborg with new
housing that blends well with the landscape* 199

Fruit of the Sea

The principal industry in Greenland is fishing. Earlier this was a second-class job left to women and hunters no longer able to hunt at sea. But now it is a job for men.

To-day, the biggest cities have large industrial plants, and in a very few years the Greenlander has made the big jump from a small one-man kayak to a cutter or trawler which can search for the fish where they are located.

For decades, the coastal fishermen have watched how foreign nations on the banks off the coast caught between 300,000 and 400,000 tons of fish annually, primarily cod. Now, however, they

Icebound shrimp cutters in Jakobshavn

Below left. The shrimps are being hauled in. Until the industrial plants had been built, supplies from the rich shrimp areas in Disko Bay had to be limited

Below right. He has earned his daily income. The salmon in his primitive canvas skiff is worth almost fifty dollars in the supermarket

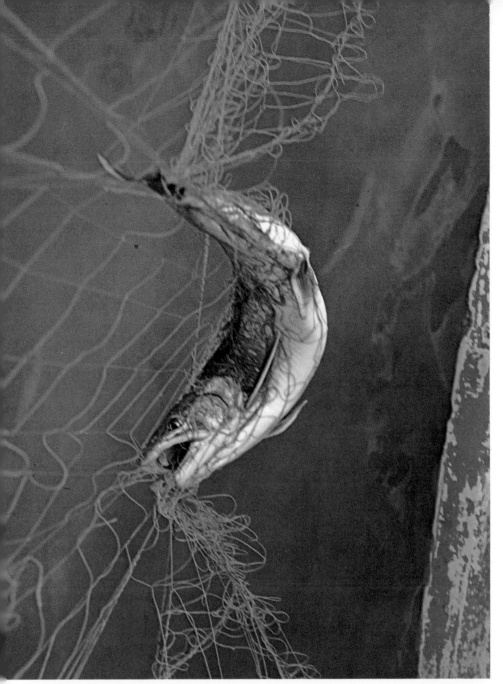

are able to take part in this competition. But during recent years the cod fishing has decreased, because of changes in the climate, and to-day the salmon fishing fetches more than the cod fishing. Four million pounds of salmon are caught annually.

A few years ago, there was not a great deal of salmon to be had near Greenland. It seems, however, as if the salmon which go out into the Atlantic Ocean from Swedish, Norwegian, Scottish, American and Canadian rivers, are dating near the coasts of Greenland.

In many countries it has aroused indignation and anger that so much salmon is caught in Greenland. One British newspaper wrote: "The Danes are a nation of rabid fishermen, no better than their ancestors, the vikings, who plundered the coasts of Europe."

Faced with these protests Denmark has agreed to limit the fishing to the same annual yield as before, even though there has never been any proof that the fishing reduced the total salmon stock.

But no one has yet complained about the fact that the Greenlanders catch 12 million pounds of shrimps in Disko Bay and in Southern Greenland, and neither have any nation offered to cover the great deficit of the fishing industry in Greenland.

Supplies for the industrial plants ashore have often been unstable just like the manpower.

Stupid to sit in a stinking factory if you can hunt reindeer inside the fjord, right?

The salmon net is tended 201

Greenland's Fauna and Flora

A group of walrus on the ice in Northeastern Greenland

Top left: Yellow puppies

Left: The polar bear is not as snowy white as many people believe

Below: Mountain hare which has never before seen a human being

Musk oxen on Clavering Island in Eastern Greenland. They are almost unconditionally protected. Only 35 may be shot annually

Far left: Angelica in West Greenland

Left: French willow in a fjord in Eastern Greenland

Below: Grouse in summer plumage

The Hunter still Hunts

On a first-time visit to Greenland–at the time of year when the country is ugliest–a Danish politician uttered these harsh words: "So, this is Greenland. A lot of rock and a lot of muck." He experienced the country during the spring thaw. The Greenland sled dogs are not that well-trained that they do their duty in certain pre-arranged spots. And when the snow–the Elizabeth Arden beauty cream of the settlement–is melting, the muck you step in, occupies your mind much more than the wonderful nature that surrounds you.

But only for a time. If you leave the settlement and its local conveniences, nature intrudes once more–moving, crushing, disarming, overwhelming.

Greenland's nature has always been called "the great, white stillness", but during the spring thaw when everything, even the brilliant plumage of the birds, begins to change, nature is in constant movement. The enchantment, which will ensure the continued existence of the species, has begun. The ringed and the harp seals, the fulmars, the razorbills and guillemots, the snow buntings, the white-sided dolphins and the piked whales are gathered in nature's horn of plenty. The hunter can draw from all this, when he leaves the small problems of the settlement behind, sailing out in his kayak and joining nature.

Even the best welfare experts would not able to create a more beautiful working place. The snow covered mountains encircle the blue, smooth water, only broken by the masterpieces designed by nature and by man–the icebergs and the kayak.

In these surroundings the hunter takes what is necessary to secure his supplies during the times of hardship when nature is inhospitable. He must keep the balance between his debit and credit account in the settlement shop, and to this end he has his kayak, his harpoon and his rifle.

However hard his life may be–he does not wish for any other.

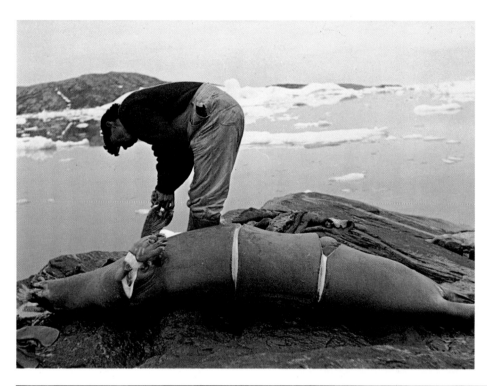

This Greenlander has just shot and harpooned a bearded seal at a breathing hole on the ice near Thule. The skin is pulled off in strips. Later it will be cut into whips, traces and lines

Modern times have been a little slow in reaching the eastern part of the country. Here, most of the people still use old-fashioned methods to earn a modest livelihood. Sometimes they are forced to go to the state welfare office, which is not always as generous as nature.
But to-day father was lucky and he is met on the beach by his wife and children. They take care of the seal, hauling it home to the wooden shack

206

He became motorized several years ago; made the jump from the kayak via the canvas skiff to the small cutter, obtained almost without down-payment and for an interest so small that you have to have a magnifying glass to notice it.

A combination of a motorized boat and a hand driven kayak is ideal in a hunting district. You are able to get out to the hunting areas quickly and safely, then you lower the kayak into the water and hunt the seal in the good old-fashioned way with a harpoon. On the way home you might even catch a little cod.

And at home, the little woman is ready with the "ulo", the special Greenland knife. She has not become motorized. She still holds the skin between her teeth while scraping it clean for blubber.

She works quick as lightning. She knows her job just as the hunter knows his

This is the way it was done 150 years ago. The same method is still in use

207

The Bloody Drama in the Fjord

Reindeer hunting is an old Greenland tradition. Even Hans Egede witnessed how the Greenlanders drove the reindeer over the steep mountain sides, so they fell down and were killed. Or they drove them out into the lakes and killed them from their kayaks. To-day the hunting is done with rifles.

For thousands of years the reindeer has been an important food supplement for all arctic people. In certain districts in Alaska up to 400,000 of these animals have been counted. Western Greenland cannot compare with this figure, but at least 5000 reindeer are shot each year, apparently without causing a decline in the population. The reindeer's worst enemies are not the rifles, but freaks of nature.

When the hunt is over the game is carried down to the cutter. If possible, this is even more exhausting than the hunt. The walk down to the coast might take several days, but what does that matter to a lucky hunter?

The reindeer is fantastically shy and alert.
Probably for very good reasons

208   *Reindeer hunt in light snowfall. The weather is calm and the reindeer has not yet scented the humans*

They fell while the summer sun was low

The boat is being filled with meat. The hunters have been lucky. The reindeer were shot close to the coast

This is the way to carry your meat and your rifle on the long marches across the mountain down to the coast

The Bear Hunt

The tales about the king of the arctic world (not the governor of Greenland but the polar bear) are as numerous as the skins adorning the arctic Eskimo's kamiks or the spot in front of the fireplace in the well-to-do homes. Each skin represents the end of a drama. Most expedition accounts have their own tale of a bear hunt, and it is almost always a bloody tale.

In an account from 1821 a British arctic explorer wrote: "From the ship we suddenly spotted a huge bear, swimming in the water. We put out a boat in order to chase it and we were only about 300 feet from it when it saw us. The bear tried to escape to an ice floe, but we cut it off and when we were 35 feet away I fired a shot which hit it in the shoulder. The big animal gave a roar and swam quickly in the direction of the boat. Furiously it tried to get into the boat or turn it over. The men pushed it back with their spears. It bit one of the spears in two. When it realized that it was not able to pull through, it sought to get back to an iceberg, despite the fact that one of its front legs was completely paralyzed. It succeeded in getting up onto the ice. I sprang after it to put it out of its misery, but I wanted to keep the beautiful skin intact and therefore walked very close to it before shooting. Suddenly, before I had time to fire, it emitted a fantastic roar and fell over dead on the ice."

The same author tells how another bear with eight bullets in its body chased four men across a mountain. In the end they jumped into the water and

A drama experienced during the German HANSA *and* GERMANIA *expedition in 1869. The man tore off his clothes a little at a time in the hope that this would delay the bear. He was not saved, however, before somebody else diverted the bear's attention*

the bear jumped after them. At the last moment, just as it was going to hit a man with its paw, the bear was shot through the head.

The Greenlanders, too, have plenty of tales about bears, but not all bears are that courageous. A man in Southern Greenland told about his meeting with a bear when he sailed the kayak mail to Sydpröven in 1920. "I had gone up onto the ice when I met a big bear. It looked at me. I aimed and pulled the trigger. But there was no shot. The rifle misfired. Now the bear attacked. I grasped

the barrel and smashed the butt right on top of the bear's head. It shook its head and ran away. Three days later I found it dead on the ice."

The Danish geologist Dr. Börge Fristrup has also told of a meeting with a bear. "We, a zoologist and I, were far up in Peary Land. One day, sitting in the tent, we discussed bears. He claimed that there were no bears in this god-

This should take place no more. The female bear has been killed and the cub is standing next to its dead mother. The picture is from 1875

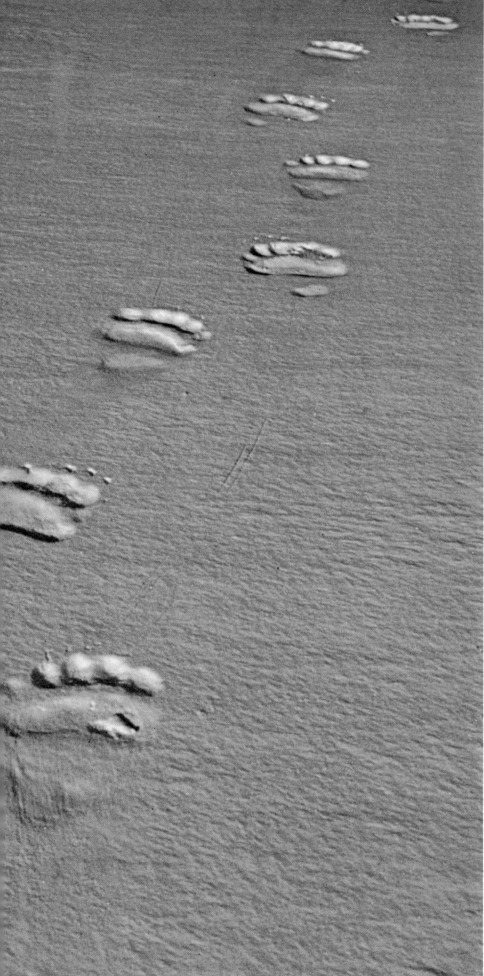

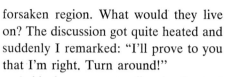
Bear tracks in the snow

forsaken region. What would they live on? The discussion got quite heated and suddenly I remarked: "I'll prove to you that I'm right. Turn around!"

A big bear was standing in the tent opening staring at us. The zoologist got so confused that he grabbed his butterfly net and started banging the bear over the head. It fled in sheer fright."

To-day all countries with arctic regions where polar bears roam have issued very strict rules on bear hunting. Female polar bears with cubs are unconditionally protected. No one knows exactly how many polar bears there are in the entire arctic world, but the number is estimated at approx. 10,000. Several countries are working together on getting the bears counted and on mapping their movements. The bears are sought out with airplanes; they are stunned with a drug bullet and fitted with a small radio transmitter which indicates their position at any time.

Dr. Börgen was not that lucky. He screamed, "Help, a bear!", when he was out for a walk only 50 yards from GERMANIA. *The bear struck him with its paw and bit him, but he was saved, nevertheless. The account of the incident paid more attention to the condition of his watch. It was found on the ice the next day, still running. German quality!*

The Art of Driving a Dog Sled

Before the dog sled is completely replaced by the snow scooter, it might be appropriate to tell what it is all about. The late Danish paleontologist, Dr. Eigil Nielsen, has given one of the best descriptions from which this is an extract:

"All of my readers probably know how a dog looks. A hairy body with a head at one end and a bushy tail at the other. The tail is the most important of the three. By watching the position of the tail it is possible, with certainty, to determine the mood of the dog. If the tail is held upright with an elegant curve over the back, the dog has no appreciable worries. If the tail, on the other hand, is sagging, it is a sure sign that troublesome personal worries weigh heavily on the dog's mind.

The dog is tied to the sled by means of a pulling rope. If you drive with eight dogs, eight equally long ropes are secured in the same spot, forming a fan and ending in a dog. To place the eight dogs in front of the sled in the correct fanshape sounds so easy and simple that anyone will be struck with consternation when he views the results of his first try. For the sake of convenience I have in the following numbered the dogs in the fan from 1 to 8, beginning at left with no. 1.

Anchoring the pulling rope to the sled does not present any great problems, however, it is advisable to start the process by securing the sled to something which cannot be moved by less than two horses.

As soon as the dogs have been placed, the following will take place: Dog 3 will jump over rope 4 and 5 and slip under rope 6 to say hello to dog 7. Dog 4 and 5 will walk with calm dignity 11 times around each other. Dog 2 will stand a moment with a deeply furrowed forehead and then he will remember that the dastardly dog 8 stole a mitten of sealskin from him yesterday. Without hesitation he pushes his way through the rope fan in order to punish dog 8. Dog 3 takes a spectator's view of the fight until he discovers that dog 8 is defeated whereupon he enthusiastically digs his teeth into the loser's left thigh. All this is contemplated with cool indifference –and through half closed eyes–by dog 1, the lead dog, while slowly lifting one hind leg in order to baptize the left runner of the sled.

The episode here described happens in less time than it takes to count to one hundred. Finally, the pulling ropes are so entangled that the dogs are unable to move a leg–unless you already have intervened with your dog whip.

A Greenland dog whip has a wooden handle approximately 16 inches long, to which is fastened a 18-24 feet long whiplash made of skin from the bearded seal. You hold the beast by the handle, swing your arm, and, theoretically, the very end of the whiplash hits firmly and forcibly the one dog in the team that you wished to punish. Practically speaking, you still hold the whip by the handle, swing your arm, and, after having described a fantastic curve through the air, the whiplash hits, not a dog, but your own face. Fortunately, I might add, this does not happen all the time. Equally often the whiplash will coil itself six times around your body, so that you can no longer use your arms, or around your legs, so that you fall and hit your forehead on the only stone sticking out of the snow within a radius of several miles."

Eigil Nielsen continues to describe

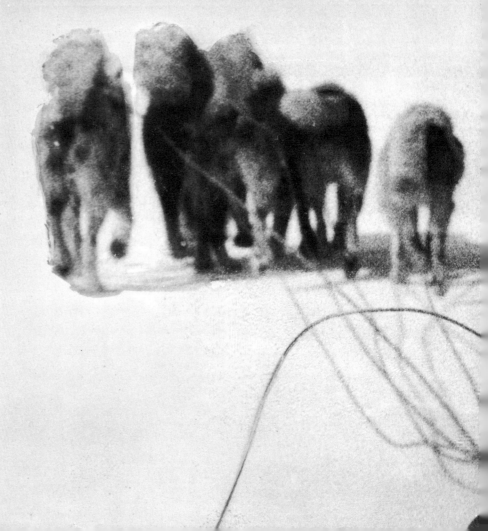

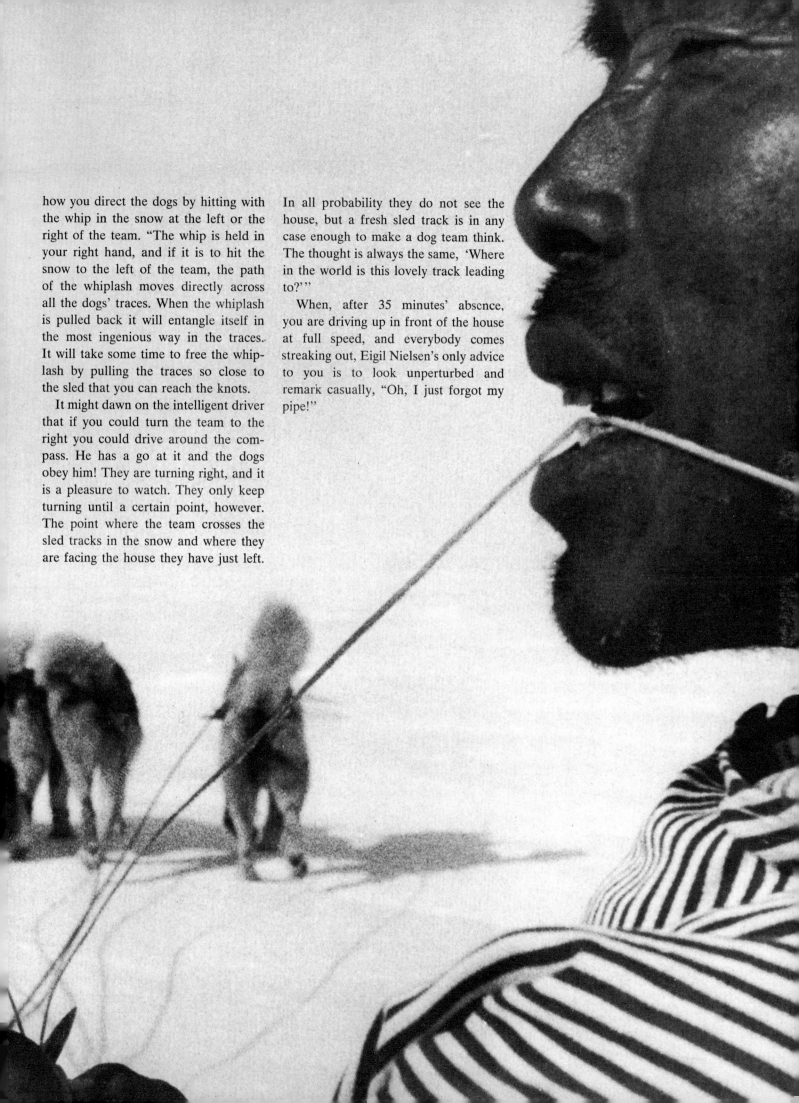

how you direct the dogs by hitting with the whip in the snow at the left or the right of the team. "The whip is held in your right hand, and if it is to hit the snow to the left of the team, the path of the whiplash moves directly across all the dogs' traces. When the whiplash is pulled back it will entangle itself in the most ingenious way in the traces. It will take some time to free the whiplash by pulling the traces so close to the sled that you can reach the knots.

It might dawn on the intelligent driver that if you could turn the team to the right you could drive around the compass. He has a go at it and the dogs obey him! They are turning right, and it is a pleasure to watch. They only keep turning until a certain point, however. The point where the team crosses the sled tracks in the snow and where they are facing the house they have just left.

In all probability they do not see the house, but a fresh sled track is in any case enough to make a dog team think. The thought is always the same, 'Where in the world is this lovely track leading to?'"

When, after 35 minutes' absence, you are driving up in front of the house at full speed, and everybody comes streaking out, Eigil Nielsen's only advice to you is to look unperturbed and remark casually, "Oh, I just forgot my pipe!"

Learning to Sail a Kayak

The Europeans of the 16th century were surprised, when they heard the accounts of the strange people, living far up north, who moved about with great speed on the ocean in small, fragile skin boats.

The kayak people has survived the vicissitudes of nature for more than a thousand years, but now they are being displaced by industrialization. Only to-wards the north and the east where time stands still, the kayak man still masters the art of turning a kayak. He is almost born with this ability, from the very first trip with his father, until the day when he gets his own "tailor-made" kayak and with his father's assistance learns to manage in all kinds of weather.

Hunting technique is part of the time table in the schools in Northern Greenland, but the art of sailing a kayak can only be learned by the do-it-yourself method.

Also, it must be learned to perfection, otherwise it might mean death. In this job people very seldom profit from their mistakes.

The oldest known drawing of a Greenland kayak. It was published in 1679 in Samuelis Reyheris' book, "Mathesis Mosaica"

214

Where Atomic Age and Stone Age Meet

The Thule Eskimos are probably the one primitive people who have taken the longest cultural jump ever. Fifty years ago these stone age people with their thousand-year old, highly developed hunting culture held the first dance on the ice with Knud Rasmussen and Peter Freuchen. To-day they live next-door to the world's most highly developed technical culture.

In 1949 Denmark became a member of NATO and two years later an agreement was signed by Denmark and the United States about the defense of Greenland. The arrangement, which may be terminated by both parties, emphasizes Denmark's sovereignty over Greenland. This had already been established at the time of the sale of the Virgin Islands in 1917. In return for the purchase the United States agreed to recognize Danish sovereignty over Greenland, including Thule and Northeast Greenland.

According to the defense agreement, the United States acquired the right to certain so-called defense areas. These are not NATO bases in the ordinary

"Mainstreet" on the Thule base with the Thule mountain in the background

The Stars and Stripes waving over a small piece of Greenland

Even radio masts have a beauty of their own, especially with the midnight sun as a back drop

The radar installation on the Thule base

216

sense, however, they were considered Denmark's principal contribution to the NATO agreement. The areas were placed at the disposal of the United States, at no cost, and the small population of hunters living near the Thule mountain were moved north to a new town, which was hurriedly built at the Americans' expense. It was called Qanaq or New Thule. The old Thule was re-named Dundas.

Thus the cold war made its entry in the cold Greenland.

The Thule hunter has a smoke before he returns home on his sled. He has been selling walrus tusks in the American barracks

Another radar network has been built across the inland ice in the South, from Holsteinsborg to Angmagssalik. Each radar station weighs 5500 tons. It is built on eight pillars, and automatically balanced from the movements of the inland ice by hydraulic jacks

A Thule hunter is picking up an old box from the American dump.
This was the kind of thing which the government thought to prevent by moving the
Thule people far away from the base

In record time a new town grew up with room for 6-7000 men and gigantic cyclopean eyes were turned towards the Soviet Union. They are as big as a football field standing on end. There are three of them plus a moveable antenna with a diameter of almost 100 feet. They have an effect of 1.5 mill. watt and are capable of detecting an object the size of a football from a distance of well over 3000 miles. In less than 14 seconds they can tell Headquarters in Colorado Springs where a rocket is fired and where and when it will hit the target. This will give the Pentagon a 13-minute respite. The radar station is being run by highly specialized technicians. Everything is automatic, but there is still need of the experts, sitting in their easy chairs, drinking tea and making notes in front of the thousand of control lamps.

The same base controls the so-called space waste, consisting of the almost 4000 pieces of rockets, run-away satellites and other space age scraps.

To-day, all civilian functions in Dundas are handled by Danish personnel, employed by an association of Danish contractors. Here, thousands of Danish workers have saved up a fortune, living a life of very reduced prices, two -three dollars for one quart of whisky, a couple of dollars for 200 cigarettes. They pay no taxes or duties. But it is a rather sexless life. Aside from a few well-guarded nurses, and the wives of some Danish telegraph operators plus a handful of imported Go-Go-girls from New York, guarded by military police –there are no women. In recent years Thule has probably lost some of its strategic importance, but nearly 2000 men are still left in this highly artificial world.

A little further north the Thule hunter continues his ancient arctic life. Of course it has been impossible to prevent all clashes between the atomic age and the stone age, in the literal sense of the word. Occasionally, a big American car has bumped into a Greenland dog sled on the ice below the Thule mountain, because the Greenland dogs are used to left-hand driving. This has been taken into consideration in the Greenland traffic laws. Cars have to stop until the dog sled has passed–on the left.

Greenland is still Greenland in the middle of a technocratic world.

A Free People

While father is out hunting, she is sewing. Here she is closing the flipper hole on a newly caught seal before she hangs the skin up to dry on a wooden frame under the ceiling. Here the skin must compete with the other decorations in the house, like clippings from magazines

The stone age is neighbor to the atomic age. The approximately 600 arctic Eskimos in the Thule district live in almost the same way as their ancestors did a thousand years ago. The basis of their existence is seal, walrus, polar bear, narwhal, fox, little auk, razorbill, kittiwake, eider and guillemot. In the most northerly district, north of the settlement of Siorapaluk, you can still find reindeer. In the rest of the district they have been wiped out thanks to the rifles which Peary gave the Eskimos when he was trying to reach the North Pole. Sea trout, Greenland halibut, arctic cod and sea scorpion supplement their daily fare. Actually, the Eskimos live in a bartering economy and their modest money requirement is covered by the sale of skins in the state shop.

This population of hunters, the most unspoilt among the 4000 Greenlanders still making a living from hunting, is well-to-do seen through the eyes of a Greenlander.

The last heathen in Thule was christened in 1926 and to a great extent the people live according to the same hunting laws which Knud Rasmussen introduced when he and Peter Freuchen settled in Thule. Here, with only 100 miles to the atomic age–the American air base in Thule–life is lived in true freedom. No alarm clock disturbs your life. Only the animals determine your travelling route and your life-rythm.

But new and different problems have invaded the Thule district. Through education in Western Greenland or in Denmark the young people have come to know an entirely different life. And they do not want to be hunters, at least not very many of them. They would rather be dressed in European type clothes, get a job in the state shop or study in Denmark.

The pictures on these pages are from the Thule still in existence, but which may disappear some day soon. The photos were taken in the fall of 1971.

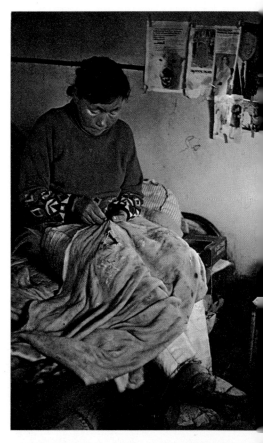

The young people do not want to stay in Thule. She is just home on vacation from the boarding school in Egedesminde

Thule's greatest bear hunter, Kangunaq, 46 years old. Every year he spends months hunting polar bears in Canada

Typical landscape in the Thule district.
At right, the Josephine Peary Island

His wife and children have been waiting
for him on the beach. The bag close to the
kayak is a white-sided dolphin

A Thule hunter returning home with
a seal. It is floating in the water

223

2000 Pounds of Meat in the Pot

On the way to the hunting area. The hunter at right is influenced by modern times. Instead of a seal bladder he has a blown up inner tube from an automobile tyre lying on his kayak

The walrus is a mountain of meat, weighing 2000 pounds or more. It is good economical food for the dogs. The meat can also be used for human consumption, however, as long as you keep away from the liver. This is so rich in vitamin A that people might become ill or even die if they eat it in great quantity. The hunters know this and do not touch it at all. Everything else on the animal can be used. The teeth are made into tools or are sold as souvenirs. The walrus might be dangerous and nowadays it is hunted from bigger boats when earlier the kayak man harpooned it from his kayak. During the winter the walrus is harpooned through the breathing holes in the ice. These photos were taken in 1971.

The walrus is hit. 2000 pounds of meat has been secured for man and beast

Walrus in sight

The harpoon is ready for the throw. If it is shot, it will sink down to the bottom. Therefore you harpoon the animal first and shoot it afterwards when the walrus is held up by seal bladders

The animal is hauled up onto the ice by the help of an old Eskimo tackle made from walrus hide. This type of tackle has been used for at least 1000 years

Flensing the walrus

A Greenland Delicacy

The fatally wounded whale is pulling the line and the hunting bladder

In the months of July and August, when the sea ice has disappeared from the Thule district, it is the open season for narwhals. The hunter keeps a look out from the coast or from the kayak, and when it is spotted, the thousand year old hunting drama begins. The hide of the narwhal is extremely tasty. It is called *Matak* and is a delicacy for the hunters and their families.

In the winter the narwhal is hunted from the ice both in Western and Eastern Greenland. The hunt is called *savssat*. If the sea freezes all of a sudden and a group of narwhals is unable to get back to the ice-free areas, the animals try to make a hole in the ice with their long tusks. The thunder they make can be heard for miles and the hunter has long ears. Then the cry "savssat" sounds, and it might be right in the middle of a sermon the pastor and everybody else run like mad to join in the hunt. A savssat may bring in as many as a couple of hundred narwhals and the winter supply is secured.

Ilenguaq, the great hunter throws his harpoon towards a narwhal

The harpoon has found its mark

When exhausted the narwhal is killed with a spear

The long haul back to the settlement begins. Four kayak men are pulling the animal

225

The City Below the Ice

Only 120 miles from the coast of Thule lies a city, dead and buried under the inland ice. It was built in 1960 down in the ice, and for two years it was the center of one of the strangest arctic experiments in our atomic age. *Camp Century* was the world's first atomic city, kept alive by a nuclear reactor and 42 pounds of uranium. The city had 21 tunnels and a main street 1200 feet long; it even had a movie theater, a canteen, water works, hobby rooms and a church room. While the snow storms were howling across the great wastes of the inland ice above, and the temperature fell to 54° below zero, the men in the city took steam baths or walked about the tunnel streets in shirt sleeves. The nuclear reactor also supplied the necessary power to keep the ice outside the tunnel streets frozen. For a period of two years 100 men lived in this city. Then it was closed down.

The main purpose of Camp Century was of a military nature, but civilians benefitted, too, from the experiment. Thanks to this atomic city, we know more to-day about the climatic development of the earth than we did previously. The Americans drilled through the inland ice and proved that it is 9000 feet deep. They fetched out the snow that fell when Jesus walked in the desert, and the snow that fell 100,000 years ago when the woolly rhinoceros and the mammoths walked about shivering on the arctic tundras of Europe.

The waste tank from the nuclear reactor is being put into place. The entire installation, weighing 413 ton, was shipped in separate parts and assembled on the spot

226

Drama over North Star Bay

An air lift was established to the radioactive ice. Here a helicopter pilot is ready for take-off

It was a little after 4 p.m. local time on January 21st, 1968. One hour before, HOBO 28, on a secret mission over the arctic regions, had refueled in the air. The co-pilot was ordered into the back to rest. The second officer took his seat. A few minutes later one of the crew reported that he could smell something like burning rubber. The captain ordered everybody to put on their oxygen masks and asked the navigator to find out what was the matter. He returned without having found anything. "Look once more," was the order. He moved a metal box and found the fire. Two fire extinguishers were emptied to no avail.

Quickly the captain called the Thule base: REQUEST PERMISSION TO FORCE-LAND. Two minutes later all lights went out.

His instant command was "Bail out".

Six of the men used their ejector seats. The seventh was doomed. The gigantic B-52 bomber was so jammed with electronic equipment that there had been no room for a seventh ejector seat. He jumped, nevertheless, but his head was crushed in the air by the falling airplane.

At 1638 hours the sirens went off all over the Thule base, but with a signal recognized only from practice training: Atomic alarm. Seconds later a mammoth crash sounded from the ice over North Star Bay.

Orange flames several hundred feet

Everybody in Thule was examined for radioactivity

The ramp to Camp Century, the city below the ice

high lit up the arctic night. The personnel at the base knew what is was. They had seen it on film: Burning hydrogen bombs.

The fire on the ice claimed the attention of the entire world. The protests poured in. Here was the proof of nuclear weapons on Danish soil, despite an unanimous parliamentary resolution against such weapons.

Trade assistant Jens Zinglersen started his dog sled and drove around to the small Greenland settlements to warn the Greenlanders not to go out on the ice.

The American government at once took immediate action. 1400 specially trained atomic renovation experts prepared to leave by jet plane for Thule.

A gigantic cleaning job began in the middle of the dark period and in temperatures down to 35° below. 67 tanks, each containing nearly 30,000 gallons of radioactive ice and snow, 3 tanks with clothing, discarded for fear of radioactivity, and 217 containers of varying sizes containing pieces of wreckage from the B-52 plane were shipped out on September 13th 1968 and later on buried in the United States' atomic cemetery.

After this, both Danish and American scientists claimed that there was no longer any danger of contamination for animals, plants or people. The American cleaning-up operation was a technical feat, but the atomic age nevertheless

had to ask the stone age for assistance.

In Thule hurricanes spring up without forewarning, and if you do not take shelter immediately you run the risk of perishing from the cold. The Americans did not dare to send the first soldiers out onto the ice, unless they had somewhere to seek shelter. Therefore, the Thule hunters were asked to build snow huts on the ice which could accommodate 100 men, and this they did. Their hand-make furs are able to withstand any storm, the same cannot be said of mass produced arctic equipment.

Later on the Eskimos probably roared with laughter in their huts over this. But people often laugh in the huts in Greenland.

227

"He is more Straightforward than our Assistant"

Greenland will probably be the last country in the world to become a republic. The population is extremely loyal to the royal family. Possibly, because it has not been overrun by kings. Greenland experienced its first royal visit in 1921, on the 200th anniversary of Hans Egede's arrival. Christian X, his queen, Alexandrine and the two princes, Knud and Frederik, were received everywhere with kayak exhibits and flotillas of umiaks and by gaily dressed Greenlanders. "He is more straightforward than our Danish assistant," one of the

Greenland women remarked about the king. And this was probably true.

It is said about the Greenlanders that they only tidy up when the king is paying a visit. This might be the explanation why they seem to be a little more orderly now than earlier, for since 1952 the king has visited Greenland four times. Usually, everything is newly painted before a royal visit. The Danish Queen knows all about that. She once tried to get too close to a picket fence with her new overcoat.

In each town a royal reception is held

for the officials, the local council, the great hunters and other dignitaries. Afterwards, the royal family hosts at a big banquet. All the dishes go out empty, at least up north, where it is common courtesy to eat up.

Speaking in terms of national politics the royal visits are of great importance because they emphasize the feeling of solidarity with Denmark. Locally speaking, they are important because a lot of Greenlanders get to speak to the members of the royal family–a wonderful topic for the long winter evenings.

Lauritz Tuxen's painting of Christian X in Jakobshavn, July 14th 1921. The illustration from a Danish satirical magazine was less pompous. "Can mommy's little seal see His Highness?"

In 1886 the first royal person, prince Valdemar of Denmark, arrived in Greenland aboard the cruiser FYLLA. It was one long gay trip. At Frederikshaab, where the colony manager sailed out to FYLLA in his kayak, dressed in tails and silk hat, a triumphal arch had been erected

A few years ago Queen Margrethe and prince Henrik visited Jakobshavn

The royal yacht among the Greenland mountains

Investing in People

Investing in people became a slogan in Greenland politics some years back.

Any young Greenlander can get very favourable loans from the state for whatever type of education he or she wishes, no matter how costly, even though higher education is not of primary importance. For the majority of the young people it is much more important that Greenland now has a technical school, a fishing school, courses for home-trade masters, typing courses, etc. More than one thousand children and young people are sent to Denmark every year to be educated.

Even though there is a teacher's college in Godthåb, Greenland has too few native teachers. A great effort is made to preserve the Greenland language and the children are taught both in Danish and in their native tongue.

Apart from their clothes they look like any other school children all over the world

The cover to the first Greenland ABC, which is called an ABD, because the Greenland language has no C.
The drawing is made by Stephen Møller

230

Morning prayers 1970 in a school chapel in the Northern Upernavik district. The teacher is not a real teacher, but a so-called "reader". He has taught himself to read and write and now he teaches the children arithmetic, writing and biblical history. Greenland has many Danish teachers, but smaller settlements still have to manage with readers

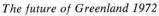

The future of Greenland 1972

Quite a few of the Greenland women work in industry. Here, they are cleaning shrimps in a fish cannery. It is quite a jump from being a hunter's wife, scraping sealskin with an ulo, to sitting in long rows in the factory in a newly ironed white smock. Not everybody considers it a step forward

Two boys on a visit back home to Thule in the summer of 1971, Otto and Paulus, both sons of hunters. Will they become hunters or city people?

Greenland's Future Lies Buried

In all probability, Greenland's future lies buried in its underground. Minerals have the advantage over fish that they do not move or disappear.

The hunt for minerals in Greenland began as early as 1606 when James Hall thought that he had found a mountain with precious ore and filled two ships with "silver". The Danish experts maintained that it was nothing but mica. Hall did not believe them and in 1612 he fetched a new load–this time financed by British merchants. It was still mica.

In 1636 when Christian IV had established a company in readiness for the whaling trade, the first two ships returned from Greenland very quickly. They did not have any whale oil in the hold, they had "gold". It was nothing but sand which was dumped in Öresund.

But other minerals have been found and utilized. Ever since 1770 Greenland has had organized coal mining, they have had a copper mine, a tin mine in Mestersvig and, above all, a cryolite quarry–economically speaking a true "goldmine". For centuries the Greenlanders have known about the cryolite near Ivigtut. They used it pulverized for sniffing as a sort of sneezing powder, and the tobacco which they bought from the whalers, was stretched by mixing it with cryolite. In 1854 the Danish chemist Julius Thomsen discovered a method whereby cryolite could be used in the production of soda and alum, among other things. In 1856 the first 100 tons of cryolite were brought to Denmark.

The deposits at Ivigtut–which are unique in the world–have been utilized for more than 100 years and are now exhausted. There are only stores left, for instance a tennis court made in cryolite, worth approx. ½ mill. dollars.

On top of a mountain in King Oscar's Fjord in Eastern Greenland very big deposits of molybdenum have been discovered. This is used, among other things, for the tempering of steel and is absolutely essential in this space age, because it is used for protection sheets for space capsules. The value of these deposits is estimated at 575 mill. dollars.

At Fiskenässet big deposits of cromite have been discovered; in Umanak Fjord a Danish-Canadian company is about to mine huge zinc deposits in a mountain called "Black Angel"; at Godthaab the Cryolite Company's geologists have found iron deposits, containing no less than two billion tons of iron ore and, finally, in Kvanefjeld near Narssaq, 4000 tons of uranium and numerous other rare and very valuable minerals have been discovered.

Whether utilization of all these finds is worth while is still unknown. It is not known either how much oil may be found in Greenland. After the enormous oil discoveries in Alaska the interest has centered on Greenland. Some of the world's biggest oil companies have tried to get concession on the research and utilization of the oil, and the first concessions will be awarded in 1972.

Apart from the economic factor, a Greenland oil adventure may have political consequences. All property in Greenland is owned by the state, the underground too. All profits go directly into the Danish Treasury. The Greenland hunter may all of a sudden discover that he is in reality an oil sheik and therefore not dependent on subsidies from the Danish Treasury. It is conceivable that his attitude toward the unity with Denmark will change. And then what?

Road signs in the middle of nowhere
on the iron ore mountain. The distance to
the inland ice is 50 meters, to Godthaab
143 kilometers and it is equally far to
Copenhagen, Helsingfors or San Francisco

Danish cryolite workers in Ivigtut at the
beginning of this century. They are
taking a smoke and drink from the bottle.
Their standard of living formed a glaring
contrast to that of the impoverished
Greenlanders

A group of barracks in the
wilderness far inside Godthaab Fjord, just
below the inland ice. The mountains
in the back contain iron ore and the
possibilities for establishing a new harbor
are being examined. The prices on the
world market will determine the start of
the project. This protograph was taken in
the fall of 1971

This is the way the cryolite quarry looks
to-day, all filled with water. Earlier the
harbor was filled with large quantities of
cryolite, but now they are scraping the
bottom

233

The Land of the Children

They were born to kamiks and seal skin, but also to rubber boots and cotton, to a childhood in a Danish-Greenland world, a mixture of old and new, poor and rich, and only subjected to the discipline which a rigorous nature imposes on everybody. What will their future be like? Will it be Danish? Greenland? European?

Their parents became wage earners with only half the average annual income of any Danish familiy in Greenland. On an average, the Danes stationed in Greenland save 15,000 D.kr. per year, the Greenlander saves 140 D.kr.

The jump from stone age to atomic age, from barter economy to money economy, from sleepy colonial times to a hectic present, was a great one and very difficult. At the beginning many stumbled. Will the children do so too? Will Danish welfare save them? Or will it make them incapable of standing up to the rough world which is their home? No one knows.

In any case, they had a better start than their parents in this Land of the People which is also the Land of the Children.

The first day of school is just as festive and just as terrifying in Greenland as in other places of the world. The mothers take their children to school and many of them are crying, because the little one is now so big that she has to leave home. That day is one of the highlights in a childs' life. Just like the first birthday. This requires a celebration. You celebrate, too, when your child has caught his first fish, regardless of the size, or when he has shot his first piece of game, even if it is only a snow bunting

The day of confirmation is another of the important celebration days in Greenland. They look a little selfconscious in their finery

The first steps are difficult, but fortunately mother is there to help you

The little one is warm and safe in the amaut, *no matter if he is sitting on the back of his mother or his big sister*

235

Illustration Credits and Copyrights

The following abbreviations are used throughout the list: AI for © *Arctic Institute, Charlottenlund, Copenhagen;* NM for the *National Museum, Copenhagen;* T&M for the *Trade and Maritime Museum, Kronborg Castle* and RL for the *Royal Library, Copenhagen.*

Key to picture position: (*T*) top, (*C*) center, (*B*) bottom, (*L*) left, (*R*) right, and combinations; for example (*TL*) top left.

Bibliography

Roald Amundsen: The North West Passage (2 vols., 1908)

Johann Anderson: Nachrichten von Island, Grönland und der Strasse Davis (Hamburg, 1746)

Bernt Balchen: War below Zero (New York, 1945)

Louis Bobé: Hans Egede. Colonizer and Missionary of Greenland (Copenhagen, 1952)

Frederick A. Cook: My Attainment Of The Pole (New York, 1911)

David Cranz: Historie von Grönland... (Leipzig, 1765)

C. H. Davis: Narrative of the North Polar Expedition, US Ship POLARIS (Washington, 1876)

The Voyages and Works of John Davis (London, 1880)

Wanda Dessau: Schleswig-Holsteins Grönlandsfahrt (Hamburg, 1937)

Peter Freuchen and Finn Salomonsen: Book of the Eskimo (London, 1962)

Jules Gourdault: Voyage au Pôle Nord des Navires La Hansa et La Germania (Paris, 1875)

A. W. Greely: Three Years of Arctic Service (1886)

C. F. Hall: Life with the Esquimaux (London, 1865)

I. I. Hayes: An Arctic Boat-Journey In the Autumn of 1854 (London, 1854)

I. I. Hayes: The Open Polar Sea (London, 1867)

Walter James Hoffman: The Graphic Art of The Eskimos (Washington, 1897)

Helge Ingstad: Land Under the Pole Star (New York, 1966)

Elisha Kent Kane: Arctic Exploration, the second Grinnell Expedition in Search of Sir John Franklin, 1853-54, 55 (Philadelphia, 1856)

J. P. Koch and *A. Wegener:* Durch die weisse Wüste. Die dänische Forschungsreise quer durch Nordgrönland 1912-13 (Berlin, 1919)

Lauge Koch: Au nord du Groenland (Paris, 1928)

Th. N. Krabbe: Greenland. Its Nature, Inhabitants, and History (Copenhagen, 1930)

Captain McClintock: The Voyage of the FOX In The Arctic Seas (London, 1859)

George William Manby: Journal of a Voyage to Greenland In the Year 1821 (London, 1822)

Ejnar Mikkelsen: Conquering the Arctic Ice (London, 1909)

Missions-Bilder (Stuttgart, 1867)

Jens Munk – An Account of a Most Dangerous Voyage Performed by the Famous Capt. John Monck In the Year 1619 and 1620

Fridtjof Nansen: Farthest North I-II (London, 1898)

Fridtjof Nansen: The First Crossing of Greenland (London, 1895)

K. Oldendow: Printing in Greenland (1959)

W. E. Parry: Journal of a Voyage for the Discovery of a North-West Passage (London, 1821)

Julius Payer: Die österreichisch-ungarische Nordpol-Expedition in den Jahren 1872-74 (Wien, 1876)

R. E. Peary: The North Pole (1910)

Carl Christian Rafn: Antiquitates Americanae (Copenhagen, 1837)

Knud Rasmussen: Neue Menschen. Ein Jahr bei den Nachbarn des Nordpols (Leipzig/Wien/Zürich, 1920)

Knud Rasmussen: Greenland by the Polar Sea (1927)

Knud Rasmussen: The Danish Ethnographic and Geographic Expedition to Arctic America. Preliminary Report of the Fifth Thule Expedition. Article printed in The Geographic Review, Vol. XV, No. 4 (New York, 1925)

Receuil de Voyages au Nord (Amsterdam, 1715)

Bernard O'Reilly: Greenland, the Adjacent Seas, and the Northwest Passage... (London, 1818)

John Ross: Narrative of a Second Voyage in Search of the North-West Passage (London, 1835)

Edward Shackleton: Arctic Journeys (London, 1937)

Vilhjálmur Stefánsson: My Life With The Eskimo (New York, 1921, ed. 1951)

Taschenbuch der Reisen (Leipzig, 1804)

John Edward Weems: Peary, The Explorer And The Man (London, 1967)

Alfred Wegener: Letzte Grönlandsfahrt (Leipzig, 1932)

Paul-Émile Victor: Man And the Conquest of the Poles (London, 1962)

Voyage Vers le Pôle Arctique (Paris, 1819)

Voyages and Travels of the Captains Ross, Parry, Franklin and Mr. Belzoni (London, 1839)

Index